The
10
Commandments
of Management

The 10 Commandments of Management

by

Malcolm Peel and Bob Norton

Illustrations by Peter Allen

C

CENTURY
BUSINESS

First published in the UK 1993
by Century Business
An imprint of Random House UK Ltd
20 Vauxhall Bridge Road, London SW1V 2SA

Random House Australia (Pty) Ltd
20 Alfred Street, Milsons Point
Sydney, NSW 2061, Australia

Random House New Zealand Ltd
18 Poland Road, Glenfield
Auckland 10, New Zealand

Random House South Africa (Pty) Ltd
PO Box 337, Bergvlei, South Africa

Set in Bembo by SX Composing Ltd, Rayleigh, Essex
Printed and bound in Great Britain by
Mackays of Chatham PLC, Chatham, Kent

A catalogue record for this book is available from the British Library.

ISBN 0-7126-5630-8

Contents

Acknowledgements

We would like to place on record our most sincere appreciation of the helpful comments a number of people have given us during our struggle with the wiles of Barripper and Relubbbus.

These include our respective wives, Nancy and Jenny, and Jonathan Glasspool, Pat Marlow, Lynn Marsh, Alison Straw and Ruth Wheatley.

In the Beginning

The letters in this book are unique. How we came by them we are not prepared to reveal, if only because to do so would cause red faces at the highest level, further resignations from government and the final collapse of the world economy. Despite protecting our source, we are under an obligation to you, the reader. It would be very easy to misunderstand what the letters can tell you and for those who do, the outlook, in this world and the next, is grim. For this reason alone, we wish to guide you in the right way to read and understand what follows.

During a recent trip to the Peak District, having ascended from Edale via Jacob's Ladder, it was revealed to us that there are Ten Commandments which those who aspire to be effective managers must know and obey. The manner of the revelation was not pleasant, but we will spare you the detail.

The text of the commandments was inscribed in a particularly complex burst of sheet lightning on a nearby boulder of millstone grit, which we attempted to remove for preservation. However, while we were carrying it down to the Edale car park, it slipped from our grasp and crashed down the hillside, smashing into a thousand fragments. One of us however, had the sense to copy the Commandments into his diary. They have thus been preserved, although you will have to take our word as to their origin.

On arriving back at Edale, we found, tucked under the windscreen wipers, a strange package consisting of ancient-seeming letters. We were intrigued to find that they were in fact based on the sacred Commandments to whose revelation we were witness.

The letters are in pairs, each pair describing in sometimes gory detail a primeval struggle between good and evil for the eternal soul of a manager. This epic struggle is fought out by a cast of characters from two camps – the Goodies and the Baddies.

The Baddies are headed by a senior member of the Lowerarchy named Barripper, who writes to a young relative of his, Relubbus, who has just been promoted to his first post as a Management Tempter. Relubbus' job is to deliver to Hades the soul of his first charge, Andrew Buckden. Barripper writes a series of letters offering advice to Relubbus on the accomplishment of this task.

Andrew Buckden experiences the problems and temptations so cunningly planned for him, and so similar to those we, and perhaps you, have experienced in our endeavours to become effective managers. He weeps, through a corresponding series of letters, on the shoulder of an older colleague whom he got to know in a previous organization.

The struggle ebbs and flows; now the forces of the Underworld seem about to triumph, now those of the glorious firmament. At one moment, all seems lost, and the jaws of Hades gape; at the next, we seem to hear the sound of angelic voices intoning the school song of the Henridge Business School. The final outcome we will not now reveal (do not turn to page 154). But as a great English writer once said, a hopeful journey is better than arrival at the eventual destination.

As the tale of Barripper and Buckden unfolds, we have included extracts of the advice given to Andrew by his remarkable helper in the hope that it will assist you when faced with similar machinations from the Underworld.

The need to share our knowledge was revealed one lunchtime when ensconced in a congenial hostelry, after our third pint of the local brew. The inspiration was, however, based firmly on one of the finest books of one of the great scholars of recent times: *The Screwtape Letters* by C.S. Lewis, to whose memory we humbly dedicate this book.

Malcolm Peel   Bob Norton

The First Letters – Self-Management

My Dear Relubbus

I was delighted to learn that you have at last aspired to the ranks of the Management Destruction Unit (MDU). To be chosen, and at such a young age, for even the most junior position within this élite corps is almost unprecedented. As you know, my own success can be said to have started when I moved to this Unit. I was personally responsible for wrecking no less than 12,560 potentially successful management careers in a complete range of industries, functions and degrees of seniority. To have the opportunity to follow in my hoofprints is the clearest demonstration yet that you are destined for the very lowest position.

I know you will be keen to start on your own duties, and I understand from the Deputy Chief Tempter that you have already been allocated to an assignment – the destruction of Andrew Buckden's management career. This is good news.

You must first understand the nature of the struggle. It is your job to deliver Buckden into the safe keeping of the Guardians of the Pit of Redundant Managers and Self-Employed Consultants. To help you are the entire resources of the Lowerarchy, subject, of course, to normal procedures, discipline and availability. In your case only, you have also the inestimable assistance of my advice. The forces ranged against you have been deeply penetrated by our agents, but are still stronger than they were. It is essential that we identify whom they have pitted against us as quickly as possible; this must be one of your first jobs.

Buckden himself will, of course, resist your efforts as best he can. His support, such as it is, must come from a medley of resources, many of which he will never be able to draw on. A range of training of various kinds is theoretically available. However, apart from its patchy quality (many trainers and consultants are either double agents or wholly in our pay), it is unlikely his employer will allow, let alone encourage, him to undergo it. There is an ever-increasing avalanche of books on management, many inspired by us. But it is likely that Buckden, like most practising managers, will have neither the time nor the inclination to read any. He may get advice from boss and colleagues, but because they will see him as a threat, any such help will be tainted. He is, therefore, for all practical purposes, on his own.

However, you can be certain that, barring most unusually good luck, the assignment will occupy your best efforts for several months. Earthly managers are ridiculously tolerant of error, especially in the young and newly-promoted, mainly because they do not like to admit they may have made a wrong choice. We in the infernal regions know better, of course, and should you fail to achieve the expected results I do not care to think of what the result for you will be.

Andrew Buckden is, as the records on the Infernal Personal Information Database (IPID) tell me, 30 years old, has a lower second class honours degree in the humanities from a polytechnic (recently created a university) a studio flat, a Ford XR3i and a live-in girlfriend. This combination should, I know, form an ideal basis for his rapid destruction, but nothing is automatic in our trade. At a later stage in the process, I know you will wish to concentrate on the various aspects of his task as a newly-appointed manager. However, my experience tells me that the best starting point in the ruin of his career is how he manages himself. It is to this area, therefore, that I intend to direct my first advice to you.

The infernal guidelines in this area are simple: **'Don't just sit there – do something!'** I suggest you start by arranging subliminal messages to this effect to be programmed into his word processor, personal stereo car tape deck and video. If you are not familiar with the procedures or technology, the Infernal Office of Misinformation Technology (IOMT) will give you the necessary help.

There is a kit of highly effective weapons available to you, and I suggest you brief yourself on their full potential and method of use immediately. A series of one-day training modules is available from the Management Section of the IOMT, and you should request a place on the next presentation of each of these through the appropriate channels. The weapons include:

- Paper
- The telephone
- The diary
- The office door
- The briefcase

You may naively believe that each of these is essential to effective management and not a weapon of destruction. Whilst there are some elements of truth in such a view, I will explain to you what the correct situation is. Let us take each item in turn.

Paper is probably the most important single engine in our destruction of effective management. Before our people invented it, our task was far harder. Managers were forced to listen to what they were told, make decisions and act on them. With each sophistication in the use of paper, we have been able to fog the issue more effectively, to the extent that many would-be managers now never see above the pile in their in-tray. The Infernal College of Mismanagement (ICM) has even popularized 'in-tray exercises' with its earthly counterparts as a serious method of training managers.

It is, as you know, an established principle within the organs of government to assess the reading capability of new members, counsellors and ministers to see that they are faced with 10 per cent more than they can read properly, thus ensuring that they allow their permanent officials to drag out any task and ensure no decisions are taken.

Make sure, therefore, that Buckden has an overflowing in-tray.

Fill it up with junk of every kind: unsolicited literature about conferences, training courses, equipment and hardware, consultancy services; personally-addressed letters from people he has never heard of; copies of minutes of meetings that are of not the slightest interest to him; internal memos about trivial administrative or procedural matters; lengthy and badly-written reports about events that happened a year or more ago; important-looking documents from government departments outlining endless and pointless new legislation: glossy brochures advertising new hotels; and free copies of newsletters. If you are successful in this, every step towards his ruination will be easier.

To make success more certain, ensure that he has several large filing cabinets and a very small waste-paper basket. I understand that he may be sharing a secretary. This is good news. With any luck, the secretary will have neither the time nor the knowledge to grasp the significance of any of this, and will place it all in Buckden's in-tray, take it all from his out-tray and file it, almost certainly in an illogical and irretrievable way.

'Information technology' is, of course, one of our biggest and most successful ploys in recent years. We put it about that electronic technology would produce 'paperless offices'. In fact we have ensured that it has produced an irresistible and ever-growing flood of paper; junk mail, memos, brochures, reports, journals and periodicals. Our back-room boys are currently working on systems for the total retention of every scrap of paper that this flood produces. The results of these are pure joy to contemplate. The costs will alone carry some organizations into bankruptcy. Should any paper requiring action, or conveying really important information, enter the system it will be immediately buried in the avalanche of junk. Knowledge that such a system exists will stimulate the further production of junk. As no one will benefit from the system it will probably chunter on for many years, fogging issues and costing money, before we replace it by an even more 'sophisticated' and useless concept.

The *telephone* is one of our best inventions. With its effective use we can ensure that a manager can be interrupted and distracted at any time. Our recent development of mobile phones has immensely strengthened the havoc we can wreak. Now not only can the manager not hide, but everyone else within earshot can also be distracted and diverted. The fact that such devices have become a status symbol has improved their effectiveness to us immensely.

Try to ensure that Buckden is allocated a car phone at once. As he is not a salesperson it can do nothing but harm. Apart from the obvious damage to his work it may, with luck, offer spin-offs such as a car accident or complications to his personal life.

Work carefully on Buckden's secretary also. With proper training by you, she can easily be convinced that she is doing the wrong thing in holding anything back from Buckden. Get Buckden to reprimand her a couple of times for not putting a call through, asking questions a caller didn't want to answer or suggesting someone else should deal with the call. If you can also ensure she is incapable of transferring calls efficiently and has a curt, aggressive manner, much will have been achieved.

Buckden's *diary* is something you will need to give attention to. To begin with, ensure that he has at least three; a desk diary, pocket diary and one on his secretary's desk. If you can slip others into his briefcase, car and home, so much the better. He will, of course, forget to transfer engagements from one to another, even assuming he enters them in any.

The permutations of this game are almost endless. See how many problems you can get him into; forgetting an appointment, double (or treble) booking, misreading date, place or time, miscalculating the length of a meeting or the time needed for travelling, etc. The achievement of young Crugmeer who, by the inspired manipulation of four diaries, produced a boardroom resignation, two broken marriages and a fatal heart attack won him, as you will know, the Golden Diary of the Year Award for last year.

Many secretaries spend much of their working day inventing and supplying excuses for managers whose diaries have led them into trouble. Someone suggested we should get a book written to help them, but it is more fun to tax their ingenuity, and quite often they end up making things worse – much worse!

For several years, the MDU worked on a device called an 'organizer', which had excellent disorganizing powers. In its basic form, it consisted of a bulky, just-portable file. It was difficult to carry, and invited managers to make a never-ending series of notes on a never-ending series of amusingly-designed forms. In many cases, we persuaded them to spend the bulk of their time completing the forms. In the later stages, MDU produced a sequence of ever more hilarious forms, to test how far they could go. From a list of deans of the principal American Colleges of management, they progressed to timetables for the 1989 spring service on the Trans-Siberian Railway, a table for conversion between Augustan and Chinese calendars, street maps of the larger towns in Papua New Guinea, a guide to the lesser known nineteenth-century vintages of the Po Valley, and a gazeteer of the Moon. Many are now valuable collectors' items.

From this, MDU progressed naturally to the 'electronic organizer'. With this they have succeeded in increasing the time taken to obtain the simplest piece of information (e.g. a manager's bookie's telephone number) by an order of magnitude. Its success as a distraction at meetings has also been excellent. Never forget the simple motto: 'The main difference between men and boys is the cost of their toys.' See what new toys you can get Buckden to find and play with.

The *office door* is a source of trouble that not every tempter uses to the full. The point is, of course, that the door must either be open or shut, and Buckden must either be behind it or not.

If it is open ('open-door management') then interruption can be arranged without let or hindrance. Buckden's chances of concentrated effort are greatly reduced. Moreover, he will have to look busy the whole time; like almost every manager he will lack the courage to sit, visible to all, thinking quietly about a problem. Never let him do this.

If it is closed, the door will cut him off from the many channels of informal communication – the overheard conversations, the comings and goings which could tell him so much. Colleagues and subordinates will be reluctant to call on him, and he will rapidly weaken his place as a member of the team, and become labelled as that ultimate of failures, a 'loner'.

If Buckden is usually to be found in his office, he will be accused of not 'walking the job'. If he spends most of his time out, he will be 'the Scarlet Pimpernel' whom everyone seeks. Vary the strategy often, and feed him plenty of conflicting advice. The scope for confusion and amusement is endless.

Have you ever asked yourself the question: 'What do managers carry in their *briefcases*?' The answer usually given in the past was 'sandwiches'. Whilst this may still be true, it is the less-credible answer 'papers' that indicates their potential destructive force. If Buckden needs a case to carry his papers, then what papers is he carrying, and why? If he is attending a meeting, it is less likely to be of value to us. On the other hand, if he is carrying the case to and from work each morning and evening, the implication is that he is taking work home; that he cannot cope during the day.

Our research indicates that managers load up their briefcases with items that (a) they are not sure how to handle, (b) think they ought to read sometime, or (c) are unhappy about throwing away. These accumulate, and will then be transferred to a larger space – perhaps a car boot or a pile in the corner of the kitchen. Should an item be needed, it will be extremely difficult to find. After a period varying from weeks to months, the whole mass will be transferred to the spare room or attic.

Those managers who are not yet fully in our clutches may summon up the courage at some stage to throw it away, but this is rare. For those who do, we arrange an immediate requirement for one of the by now missing documents, preferably from their Chief Executive. More frequently, we are able to persuade managers that they need ever-bigger briefcases, sometimes combined with a filing cabinet in their home.

This would be fertile ground for our plans. Work on it; there is no limit to the harm you can do. Make him believe taking work home regularly is the hallmark of a conscientious manager – even a status symbol – and within a year you may have the pleasure of seeing him dying from a heart attack or crippled by excessive drinking!

Needless to say there are many other aspects of Buckden's self-management that can help in his destruction. A common and today more fruitful hunting ground is the conference and course scene. Get Buckden to attend as many of these as possible. Ensure that he sees lunch and dinner times as convivial occasions, and feed him the old chestnut that 'the most useful time on any course is round the bar in the evening'. If you work at this, it should be possible to have him stay up till one, two or even three o'clock each night and believe it shows what a promising manager he is.

Try to fog his assessment of priorities; this can be an endless source of amusement. Our best operators can get a manager running round in circles completing his boss's monthly report while the place is on strike, or refining a design detail of next year's model while a key customer is threatening to transfer business to a rival. The most impressive piece of work was by old Croglin, who got his manager to ignore the fire alarm and sit in his smoke-filled office finalizing his revised budget submission. All they ever found were the steel rims of his spectacles.

The reports available from IPID on Buckden's girlfriend are not yet complete. Depending on what they come up with, there may be scope for a little sexual harassment by Buckden; our Sexual Interests Directorate will advise you. At the worst, you can arrange for her to keep him in bed in the morning, or set up some nasty, emotionally-disturbing rows.

I have saved the best news for you until last. It so happens that I planted a sleeper in Buckden's firm several years ago; a reliable agent with the codename Srebmun. I am making arrangements to activate him. If he is vetted positive, I will inform you of the address of the dead letter-box and the call and answer codes in the usual way. Use

Srebmun well – he could be the key to your success. I am also having my people make enquiries about a double agent known to us as The Curate.

Keep me in the picture.

Your loving uncle

Barripper

Garden Flat
Bristol
Wednesday 15 January

Dear Michael

How marvellous to hear from you after all this time. It must be at least four years since we were last in touch. It's an amazing stroke of luck that you should write – I was recently appointed to a general management position with United Group plc, (you've probably heard of them – they manufacture garden figurines) an important career step for me.

My title is Company Projects Manager. I've got a company car, a secretary, an office with two telephones – blue for internal and red for external calls – and a microcomputer linked into the network.

The advertisement spoke of my job as 'a key post in a vibrant young team', but I must admit I'm still not sure what it meant. I see myself as a kind of trouble-shooter, I think, although I had expected a more detailed briefing when I started. My boss, Peregrine Hines, has the title of 'Comptroller'. He took me to my office, and sat down in my chair. Unfortunately the blue phone rang and he was called away just as he was about (I presume) to brief me, and he hasn't been able to spare time since.

My job description gives me plenty of scope.

- Reporting as required to the Comptroller on the organization, implementation and effectiveness of company projects.

- Internal and external liaison.
- Ensuring efficient objective-setting and planning in effective project development.
- The exploitation of resources in undertaking all projects.
- Monitoring, controlling and leading project teams to a successful conclusion.

All this looks fine, but I'm beginning to see problems ahead. The world of management has come to me as a shock – either the organization is in a mess or I am. I feel pressure to 'get on with it', but I'm not sure exactly what 'it' is. The checklist you sent me is just what I need; you must be psychic.

Yesterday, I arrived at my office with the in-tray filled higher than ever. The blue telephone rang almost continuously for twenty minutes while Joan, my secretary, was putting calls through to the red one without asking who was calling or why.

I was on both phones at once when Alan Bowden, the Financial Accounts Manager, appeared for the 'nine-thirty appointment I had made'. I'd forgotten he was coming, but we were both taken aback when Joan shouted through that a visitor from the Association of Project Managers was on his way from reception to see me. On checking my pocket diary, I found that I had indeed asked him to come. The diary was still open in my hand when Joan put through a call from someone who wanted advice on whether a leaving present would be more appropriate than a visit to the pub in reward for five years' service. What did I think? I blew my top. Alan left saying he'd call back later.

I asked Joan to dig out my notes for the meetings. After several minutes scrabbling in trays and filing cabinets, she came in with two handsful of everything except what I needed. How she had filed it defeats me. It defeated her too.

I took the meetings one after the other. I found them unsatisfactory and unproductive. I know my visitors felt so too. I spent lunch-time hunting for papers which should have been in my briefcase and the afternoon picking things out of my in-tray, wondering what value they could be to anybody.

On my way home a message on my car phone told me that there was no OHP available for my evening presentation. I went straight through a red light on hearing that one.

Without the OHP the presentation was a disaster. Back home, Laura and I had a bitter row about the heaps of paper I leave everywhere. Laura gave up on me, and this morning I woke in the armchair, papers still strewn everywhere.

The look Laura gave me as I left that morning made me realize that I needed to sort myself out. I think you called it 'personal effectiveness'. I never considered the need to manage myself before; I suppose I thought that I was above that kind of thing.

Yesterday, I stumbled on an article in a newspaper I found on the train. Oddly enough it had been removed from my office copy. It said that most of us were bad at managing ourselves, our time and our paperwork. The article caught my attention before your name hit me; you seem to be shadowing me somehow, at the moment! In any case, your article described me to a tee.

You say that we – I – should be doing one of three things when paper hits the desk: act on it, pass it on or bin it. It really struck a chord. I've the smallest of waste-paper baskets and that's where most of it belongs. A lot of it should never have come to me in the first place.

I realize now that my secretary is a key player in this; I'm lucky to have one to myself. I'd not realized how much we need to work together. I must come to an understanding with Joan on how we should handle my mail. I think it would be best if she were to screen everything. I realize now that I get at least as much junk mail in the office as I get at home; advertising matter, unwanted reports, copies of internal memos 'for information' – what you will. We must sort out the filing system too.

Joan and I can plan the diary a week in advance and check it at the beginning of each day. If we both know my priorities then we'll avoid the shambles that is beginning to take over.

Joan can help me in lots of other ways as well. I think that my outside phone calls should come through her. The red phone can go:

the wretched gadget seems to know when meetings reach a critical point. I'm also getting rid of my car phone. It may be useful to some, but to me, it just delivers extra problems.

I've given serious thought to the amount of work I am taking home. We all do it now and again: I've started doing it every night. It's got to stop: with better management of my office time, I'm sure it will.

Evening courses and weekend conferences seemed a great idea in the beginning. Mr Hines has been prepared to sign me up for any I fancy. But already I find it impossible to remember what most of them were meant to be about. All I actually remember is the bar and the jokes. Last week, at Henridge, the stories went on all night.

Your letter and Laura's common sense have given me a new perspective of the balance I need. I'm going to rejoin the Rugby Club. Laura can see me in action in the scrum for a change.

Michael, it's not too late to make a fresh start, is it? If I can't get myself organized there's little hope for anything else.

Yours sincerely, if four years late . . .

Andrew Buckden

Extract of a letter from Michael Temple to Andrew dated 8 January

. . . if you manage to apply these measures of self-discipline, they should lay a solid foundation for organizing your time. Here's a summary of the points you should try and keep in mind.

- Organize your time by setting priorities in advance and by asking your secretary to help you keep a methodical diary. If you have more than one diary, transfer appointments methodically.
- Remember that your secretary can be your greatest help, but do not overburden her with petty rules and requests. Work together as a team and ensure you know each other's way of working.
- When organizing your day make sure you have time to be

available to others, but make sure equally that you have freedom from interruption when you need it. Few managers ever succeed in this but it is the key to getting things done. One trick is to build in 'blanks', or spare time, between meetings.

- Don't place too much reliance on gadgetry. Technology is increasingly cheaper to come by, but it can rule you unless you know how to control and exploit it. Beware of too many telephones, and too much uncoordinated electronic support. Only use it if it really helps.
- Dispose of paperwork when it has been acted upon unless there is a valid reason for keeping it. Remember that the filing cabinet industry is booming from too much computer printout. Do not pass papers on to others unless you know there is a need. Passing the buck creates unnecessary work and does not solve problems.
- Beware of taking work home regularly; see it as a danger signal and examine the cause. Keep a sense of balance. Follow the 'Mars Bar' approach and allow time for work, rest and play.

THOU SHALT ORGANIZE THYSELF AND SET A GOOD EXAMPLE TO OTHERS

Michael

The Second Letters – Planning and Objective-Setting

Dear Relubbus

I have to say that I was not as pleased as I would have liked by the reports of the first phase of your assignment to destroy Buckden's management career. The Watchers have reported that, despite your efforts, he has gained some control over his own work, and is even keeping an effective diary and setting sensible priorities. Your tradecraft is deficient at the moment; the removal of the article from his newspaper was naive and only served to draw his attention when he saw it later. It is also due to your ineffective planning that he now has a full-time secretary.

I am aware, however, that this is your first assignment, and provided all goes badly from now on nothing will appear on your personal file. Luckily for you, the second phase is one of the juiciest, and if well handled can lead to immediate disaster for Buckden. I am also informed that the agent Srebmun is suitable for activation. Make contact (through dead letter-box UT3186Z) at once. Double agent The Curate is to undergo a polygraph test; I will let you know the result in due course.

One of the clearest signs of effective management is skill in planning. The chances that Buckden will prove an effective planner are, mercifully, slight. Few managers enjoy planning, and even fewer are good at it.

Ineffective managers are forever overtaken by events and spend the great bulk of their time 'fire-fighting' as they picturesquely call it. (Of course their experience of fires is extremely limited, and of little help when they eventually join us and are faced with the real thing.)

Whatever name they give it, bad managers spend their working lives being surprised by events, having their priorities upset, and staggering from one crisis to another. They think this is in the nature of management – some glory in it and feel it justifies their existence. We know it happens because their planning is deficient.

There are seven tools in our Planning Destruction Kit. They are:

- Getting stuck in
- Mumbo-jumbo
- The crystal ball
- MBO
- Budgets
- Project Planning Mayhem (PPM)
- The fire extinguisher

(The up-to-date training programme of the ICM will tell you when the next presentation of each of these modules is due.)

Managers love to *'get stuck in'* (or 'go for it' in the latest jargon) straight away; this is one of their favourite sayings. Faced with whatever situation, from a normal day's work to a major new project, they see themselves as shirt-sleeved, let's-cut-the-cackle people. They describe anywhere except the field of action as 'the ivory tower' or 'the palace of varieties'. Their fingers itch to handle what they feel is the stuff of real life, and they boil with impatience at the thought of mere thought.

Planning certainly delays the start of the action. Ensure Buckden sees this as a problem. Make him feel that time thinking is time wasted, and that managerial machismo calls for instant decisions and ruthless, incisive implementation. Let Buckden see using time for planning as an admission of failure.

As he is a young thruster, this may not be difficult; his instinct will be to rely, like many young motorists, on the speed of his reactions. Just as they enjoy the thrill of danger, so a young manager can be made to enjoy coping with hazards, rather than planning to avoid them. His motto should be: 'Don't confuse me with the facts – my mind's made up.'

As in other areas, *mumbo-jumbo* is one of our most powerful tools. The ICM has unparalleled expertise in its manufacture. Feed him the conviction that planning is a job for the experts, strategic planners, project directors and so on. Never let him realize that plans can be as simple or as complex as the occasion demands, and are always best made by those who will have the responsibility for carrying them out.

Ensure he has heard of all the variations of network analysis – PERT, CPM, etc. – and believes they are highly technical and only for use by specially-trained boffins on large projects. Operational research is a good area for confusing him. Let him hear about Linear Programming, the interpretation of duality, complementary slackness, Dijkstra's algorithm, deterministic inventory control, two-bin policies, the negative exponential distribution, the Poisson Process, terotechnology, random event structures, Games Theory, Minimax, Queuing Theory, simulation, modelling or what you will, provided he does not fully understand or get value from any of them.

The ICM has a thesaurus of these things; make sure you get a copy. It is continually adding to the list to ensure that nothing settles down. The ICM will also tailor-make techniques or terminology to confuse individual situations or specific managers. However, I would recommend you not to experiment with these more expensive and advanced methods yet. There is a simple do-it-yourself technique deviser, based on a well-known approach pioneered by IOMT which is more appropriate for your present level of skill. The deviser produces a new technique by the use of any combination of three digits in conjunction with the following table:

The infernal technique deviser		
1. Random	1. Replacement	1. Algorithm
2. Standard	2. Exponential	2. Modelling
3. Discounted	3. Graphical	3. Programming
4. Complementary	4. Probability	4. Analysis
5. Linear	5. Factor	5. Formulation
6. Iterative	6. Resource	6. Distribution
7. Deterministic	7. Parametric	7. Series

Thus, you may suggest to Buckden that he should be aware of the value of (1,3,5) 'Random Graphical Formulation', or should look up the (6,5,4) 'Iterative Factor Analysis' technique before finalizing any plans. It has been said that 7.4.4. caused the recession of the 30s and a virtual certainty that 7.4.2. caused the Stock Market Crash of 1987, one of our greatest successes.

Our next weapon against planning is what we call the *crystal ball syndrome*. Time is more of a problem for human managers than for us in the Lowerarchy; they are actually unable to see ahead at all. In their attempts to overcome this they adopt a range of extraordinary and ineffective stratagems, most of which have, of course, been devised by us. Because he cannot see into the future, Buckden, like others, may become fascinated by hints that he might.

There is a range of attempted methods of seeing into the future to which the ICM has succeeded in attaching full credibility. Some would, if we were to leave him alone, help him. The trick is to ensure that he does not understand their strengths or limitations but believes that a nodding acquaintance with them is a form of one-up-manship that will impress his colleagues.

In this spirit, let Buckden hear of the Delphi technique, linear regression, Box-Jenkins . . . anything that leaves him feeling that he can see what tomorrow will bring.

Like many before him, your man may become obsessed with statistics. At the simplest level, he may fall into the error of projecting trends into the future – a rising curve must go on rising, a fall will go on falling. For variety, suggest that a strongly-rising curve must indicate an incipient fall, or vice versa. You may have difficulty in believing such simple traps could work, but they have been responsible for some of the worst management errors ever made.

The most fruitful field for the crystal ball is in personnel selection. As we all know, predicting human behaviour, especially in the context of a new job, is impossible. However, Goulceby has succeeded, after several decades' work, in persuading many otherwise rational managers that it is possible to devise tests that will do just this. He has hidden the fact that, even if a test can place humans into psychological categories (and there is little agreement on what these may be), this cannot forecast how they will behave. Goulceby's weapon is the sense of magical power such a supposed method of forecasting gives. His latest breakthrough is to convince many managers that graphology can do the trick. He tells me that his next project will be a revival of phrenology.

One of the finest achievements of the MDU, back in the late 1950s, was to ensure that *Management by Objectives* (MBO), which had been a dangerously useful approach, became bogged down in mountainous paperwork. MDU's agents did well, and few now use MBO. The setting of objectives is the most basic (and, if we were to let the truth out, the most useful) form of planning. Work to ensure Buckden gets no value from this all-too-sensible technique. You might start by confusing him with terminology. Get him arguing whether something is an 'objective', an 'aim', a 'goal' or a 'target'. If you can find one or two colleagues for him to play it with, this game can last for hours, and generate real bad blood.

Next, work up the complexity and the bureaucracy of the concept. Get him to see objectives as things that are tied to an annual, paper-bound system of appraisal, or that can only be set by the Board.

Whilst working on MBO, we made the art of setting objectives appear harder than it is. We know that sensible objectives must neither be too demanding (or undemanding), too long-term or too vague and unmeasurable. But while some managers see them as the opportunity to create unattainable daydreams, others are so frightened of failing that they call for no exertion whatever.

Budgets offer a goldmine of problems. Buckden will in any case hate everything about them. He will shudder at the word, and try to hide when the paperwork first arrives in his in-tray. He will prevaricate as long as possible, pretending he has lost the documentation or does not understand it.

When at last he has been got moving, the fun really starts. He will fail to tie in his budget with any plans he or anyone else has (despite your efforts) managed to formulate. He will bid for more resources than he can justify, on the basis that his bid will always be reduced by senior management. There will be conflict with other managers whom he will see, probably correctly, as rivals. He will forget the implications of new markets, products and methods on his capital requirements. He will be over-optimistic about sales. Ensure he also underestimates costs.

May I remind you of the Six Stages of Project Planning Mayhem (PPM):

1. The selection of the Unworthy
2. The planning of the Unworkable
3. The briefing of the Unwilling
4. The harassing of the Confused
5. The persecution of the Innocent
6. The promotion of the Ineffectual

Here also, don't underestimate human stupidity. The fact that a committee of experts has been called together guarantees nothing.

Indeed, there is evidence that the more experts involved, the greater the scope for disaster. It will be a year or two before Buckden reaches this league, but even in his present position he will be able, with your guidance, to do a lot of harm.

Our research has established that most plans start either too far back (what everyone wanted to do fifty years ago) or too far forward (what they think will be needed in a hypothetical future). If you get the chance with Buckden, choose one of these scenarios, and play it for all you are worth. Call in at the MDU Planning Bureau where you will see bridges that were not needed, roads that were choked with traffic the day they were completed, offices that have stood empty since completion, planes that flew once only and river barriers whose only use is to attract tourists.

The need for coordination will generate a battery of harmful pressures and temptations. To get the project agreed, Buckden, like anyone else, will underestimate costs and the time for completion.

Immediately on receiving this memorandum, check Buckden's *fire extinguishers*. Make sure he finds them empty or in other ways unusable. Few managers ask 'What if my plan goes wrong?' For one thing, managers assume their plans are perfect; for another, they feel uncomfortable in facing the prospect of potential problems. Your job is to ensure that he does not ask this question; if he were to, he might take rational preventative action, or even set contingency plans.

Tell him that when the plan is complete, it is sure to work. This way, every problem will come as a shock. Not only will he spend his time fire-fighting, but he will have to do so with an empty extinguisher.

Let me know how you get on!

Uncle Barripper

Garden Flat
Bristol
Friday 31 January

Dear Michael

Thank you for your letter and the second checklist. It has already proved its worth, as I shall describe. You seem to have a telepathic understanding of my problems!

Yesterday, I arrived at my office to find two books on my desk. One was called *Network Analysis and Corporate Planning*. The other was a mix of initials called OR, PERT and PPM. I wondered if Mr Hines could have left them as a guide as to what he wants me to do; I'm beginning to feel even less certain what that is. The books only raised more questions. I thought back to our discussions but Linear Resource Modelling was a new one on me. Do other managers plan in this way? I went home feeling that if this was what planning was all about, it may not be for me.

As Project Manager, it seems to me that planning has got to be part of my remit, even though Hines has not explained what my involvement should be. With my personal time more under control, I decided to visit one or two of my colleagues to see how they went about it.

Jim, the Production Manager, had both phones off the hook when I walked in. There were three people in his office, and he was carrying on four conversations at once.

'You want to talk about planning . . . ?' he started gloomily, when they had gone.

There was a bang on his door and a head poked through.

'Feeder's down again, Jim,' said the head.

'I'll be with you in a moment,' said Jim wearily as it disappeared.

As I tried to explain that I was wondering how planning was done in Production, another head appeared with the message that a schedule had arrived from Computing with several physical impossibilities in it. Jim picked up the phone and had a five-minute shouting-match with the IT Manager. The second he put the phone down, it rang again. It appeared that the packing machine had developed a defect with the wrapper.

'Management have known about that machine for years,' said Jim, with a shrug of his shoulders.

The phone went again. 'It's a real emergency, this one,' he said. 'Shop steward's calling them out – too many breakdowns.'

'Planning is what we don't get time for here,' he shouted back as he walked out.

Sue in Marketing was working on her micro, an impressive machine with a tower at one side and a display of flashing lights.

'It's a 486S EX,' she began, 'but they wouldn't let me have the software I wanted.'

She showed me some printouts.

'As you can see, I've used a fairly simple model based on the Nyquist frequency for this,' she explained.

I nodded sagely.

'It proves that we should base our marketing strategy on the preferences of the c – d younger marrieds. On the other hand,' she continued after a pause, 'When you consider the relationship between the periodogram and the covariance function, there is clear evidence that a better strategy would be to aim for the expanding market of the "new" pensioners.'

In an attempt to relieve the intellectual pressure, I asked how often she got to see Jim in Production.

'In the quarterly meetings and at Christmas' she replied briskly. She was in no mood for conversation, and turned back to her pc.

I was on the point of leaving when she cried out 'Eureka!'

This was clearly the one she had been waiting for. To me, the printout looked like a terminal case of hiccups.

'That's it. By transforming the truncated covariance function with simple spectral analysis, you can see that the growth pattern for the next three years is unbroken. It's got to be the younger married market.'

'What data are you using?' I asked cleverly, as I thought.

'Population and income statistics over the last decade,' she exclaimed with a 'What else?' note in her voice.

I was on dangerous ground: 'Isn't that placing too much reliance on a limited set of past figures? Don't we need one or two other inputs, maybe from the experienced members of the sales force?'

Sue replied curtly that we had spread our marketing resources too thin for too long. I took the hint, and left quietly.

I had a hidden agenda for my visit to Arthur Harris in Admin and Office Systems. The office I have been given is in the East Wing, and I wanted an office nearer the Marketing and Accounts in the central complex. My request met with a knowing, almost condescending reply; A & O would get to it in due course. I asked when. Arthur explained that a complete office re-organization scheme was in progress; it had been in progress for as long as he had been there. I explained that I only needed to be nearer to one or two colleagues with whom I had regular contact. Everything was in hand, he said patiently. I persisted, and after a while he produced a scale model of the latest proposals. He barked a message to an invisible subordinate named Martin to add my name to future circulation lists. I had heard of Martin as one of our brightest prospects and it was no secret that Arthur kept him firmly in check. I asked Arthur what was behind the reorganization. He explained that one of Hines' first acts had been to call in a consultant to review the situation. I asked what the reorganization was intended to achieve and found myself embroiled in a heated discussion on the differences between 'aims', 'objectives', 'goals' and 'targets'. I asked if Heads of department had been consulted, but he was saved by the phone.

I thought I would get some common sense from Alan in Accounts. He was a down-to-earth Yorkshireman who had been in the post for some years. I found him with his feet up on his desk.

'Busy?' I asked, with a faintly sarcastic smile.

'As a matter of fact, yes,' he replied.

I explained the reason for my visit.

'Planning' said Alan, 'sure, that's just what I'm doing right now.'

He was thinking about a request from our boss. In order to project forecasts for the next three years with greater accuracy, Mr Hines wanted to move from cost to inflation accounting.

'Will that do what he wants?'

'Not really,' said Alan. 'Any system is only good as the figures going into it, and most of them are duff. Well not duff exactly, but based on the past, and then projected to the future. That makes it a "forecast", but at the best it's only clever guesswork. We don't really know what's going to happen tomorrow: a rise in the interest rate, Stock Market jitters, widening of the trade gap – it can all change at the drop of a hat. Systems don't provide answers. They can only provide suggestions, and then only if the data and the programme are sound and the conditions are the same as when the data were compiled . . .'

'So what are you going to tell Hines?' I asked.

'That his idea is a waste of time.'

I risked a suggestion: 'Surely sound information can provide the basis for good planning?'

Alan nodded. 'Of course. The problems come when people assume that, just because they have used a computer and a few sophisticated techniques, forecasts are reality. In my experience, that happens most of the time, and I sense more than a touch of that in the way Hines put his request.'

I thanked Alan for his time and left him to his thinking. Of all the people I met that morning, he was the only one whose approach to planning seems sensible. Seeing how my colleagues plan makes me wonder if people know what they are doing next, or why. But it has given me some ideas to discuss with my boss, if I can get through to him. Hines seems to be a remarkably busy man.

I look forward to hearing from you again. I wonder what problems you will anticipate for me next time.

Best wishes

Andrew

Extract of letter from Michael to Andrew dated 25 January

. . . so that when you get down to it, planning must come first. Do not, as many have done, ignore its importance. Your Production Manager, Jim, will need a lot of support in planning to overcome the obstacles that face him. I sense too that the Admin function may play a large role in the way you plan ahead, although you must be wary of some people's tendency to side-track you. Without planning, there is no way to check how well you are doing and no basis to measure what you achieve. As before I'll summarize the main points I've been making:

- First and foremost, do not be frightened of being 'caught out' in the act of thinking. It may well look as though you are doing nothing but it should not be necessary to provide a disguise for thinking.
- Be patient and allow time for planning, even for simple things, and set clear objectives for every activity.
- Make allowances for the human elements, or human failings, when and wherever your plan may be affected. Remember that without the cooperation of your people, any plan is certain to come to grief. Involve the key people in your team from the outset.
- It will now be obvious that too many top-down plans are ill-conceived. They falter without consultation and input from those applying them. Remember that without bottom-up communication, plans become 'instructions' which wither and die along the way.
- Managers are not clairvoyant and do not have the power of the crystal ball. Never believe that you can see into the future with certainty whatever techniques you may use. Allow for contingencies and be prepared to use your own judgement and common sense. Don't let systems or procedures take over.
- Be wary of too many estimates and guesstimates dressed up as forecasts or projections. Most of them are based on what's happened in the past without any guarantee that they can

provide anything more than useful experience. Always provide contingency actions against problems or failures.

- You can do worse than remember the words of Harold Wilson who said: 'I'm an optimist, but I'm an optimist who always takes his raincoat . . .'

THOU SHALT SET OBJECTIVES AND PLAN WITH CARE

Michael

The Third Letters – Communication

Relubbus

Once again, I have to say that the reports about your work are not encouraging. He seems to have avoided such traps as you laid for him, and come to some ridiculously sensible conclusions about the planning methods of his colleagues. Leaving books on Buckden's desk was crude and bound to be ineffectual. Is this really the quality of tradecraft now taught at ICM? I do hope it will not prove necessary to send you to an Infernal Reassessment Centre. I also await any indications you have of the identity of the forces ranged against us. You must work on this urgently; put pressure on The Curate to tell us what he knows. Buckden is getting help from somewhere.

Fortunately, The Curate has passed the polygraph test. However, he is cleared only for Level 3 use. You will know what this means by reference to your ICM Security Codes manual.

However, to move on. You will frequently hear managers claiming 'Our communications are bad', 'We have a communications problem' and similar sentiments. You may think that this displays insight, and must make our task harder. In fact, thanks to some superb work by Buttercrambe, Dean of Miscommunication Studies at ICM, the opposite is the case.

Buttercrambe has ensured that the word 'communication' has become the all-purpose excuse. Any kind of management failure may be explained as a 'failure of communication'. This can explain a

strike, loss of an important customer, failure to meet a sales target, or a major design error in a new product. The words have become a magic formula that does away with the need for thought or action.

From this starting point, Buttercrambe has produced total confusion. By 'failure of communication' some managers mean that the telephone system is out-of-date and the telephonist rude; others, that the organization structure doesn't work; others again, that 'people don't talk to me much', that the fax is always breaking down, or that people won't do as they are asked.

Human communication, such as it is, takes place in several ways; face-to-face, in writing, in meetings, by telephone, by machines such as faxes, telexes and computers, and by telepathy. All offer scope for mischief; here are one or two ideas.

Face-to-face

Most managers love the sound of their own voice. They talk when they should listen, sound off about things they do not understand, interrupt in meetings and interviews and develop incurable verbal diarrhoea. Ensure that Buckden never thinks before he speaks. With guidance, he will soon get a reputation for rudeness and lack of thought.

Many years ago, Buttercrambe concluded there was a danger that the concept of 'body language' might become too useful. Working with young Thorngumbald, he succeeded in relegating it to a form of superstition, alongside phrenology and palmistry. Here are one or two extracts from their latest guide to the subject:

- A subordinate waving clenched fists and with an aggressive facial expression suggests that the manager should find urgent business elsewhere.
- A colleague standing on the roof with one arm vertically above the head and the other at right angles on the left indicates that the phone is u/s and semaphore is being tried.
- Violent twitching of the skin above the right eyebrow indicates a desire to go to bed with the other party, unless that is the

Management Accountant, when it suggests that the expenditure budget has been seriously exceeded.

- The raising of index and middle fingers, especially with thumb between, suggests a degree of unhappiness or potential disagreement with an instruction.
- Heavy breathing, especially if combined with closed eyes, suggests that the individual is asleep unless combined with low moans, in which case a degree of sexual harassment may be suspected.
- Scratching of the left backside during a briefing session indicates an itch.

Work on timing. Get Buckden to broach important discussions when people are desperate with hunger or bursting for the WC. Tempt him to summon supervisors for their annual appraisal at the end of a hectic day, when the production line is down or as they are packing up for a fortnight's leave.

Stress is a useful tool. Ensure that Buckden asks his subordinates to produce a detailed business plan for a new project the day before their youngest child is about to go into hospital or, failing that, when their partner has just left them for another.

In writing

One of our most powerful strategies was blown by the enemy agent who first told humans that: 'Man invented language to hide his thoughts.' Luckily, few managers have heard or understood this. As a *recent* graduate in the humanities, Buckden's linguistic skills are likely to be wishy-washy at best and impetuous at worst. To make his writing even less effective (if that is possible), here are one or two ready-made suggestions from Buttercrambe's invaluable *Dictionary of Managerial Misusage*. Try hypnotic suggestion just before he begins writing, or programme subliminal messages into his word-processing software:

- Use long, complex sentences in which the number of

subordinate clauses and adjectival, noun or adverbial phrases is endless and the construction becomes completely lost both by the reader and the writer, preferably running to a length of at least thirty words (bear in mind that the record, established in 1971 by a manager shadowed by Buttercrambe himself, is no less than two hundred and fifty-six words without a full stop).

- Choose splendiferous and awe-inspiring terminology, preferably employing linguistic expressions with which the average reader is likely to be unfamiliar. A spade, for example, should become 'manually-operated horticultural excavating technology'.
- Sprinkle adverbs liberally, abundantly and altogether very confusingly.
- Use many protracted, idiosyncratic, ineffectual and superfluous adjectives.
- Use punctuation at, random especially commas,

Try to ensure he always works at the last minute, and never sees the evil advice 'If I'd had more time, I would have written less.'

Self-importance is a great weapon in producing turgid prose and meaningless waffle. Tell him he must 'impress rather than express'.

Anger can be helpful. If someone, especially a customer, upsets him with rude letter, ensure that he immediately sends back an even ruder riposte. I love to see such a letter lying on the Chief Executive's desk as a manager is led trembling into the room.

Meetings

Regular meetings are a form of ritual torture managers inflict on one another that give a foretaste of what we have in store for them.

Buttercrambe has written up some fascinating research into meetings at the time of the Druids based on runic inscriptions he discovered on one of the sarsens at Stonehenge. During the building, the High Priest, on the second Thursday of each month, would confine his deputy project managers in a nearby hovel with lists of the latest shortages of material and slaves, stoppages and corrections.

As the schedules and critical path had been based on a faulty observation of the winter solstice, the meetings got longer and more tense, whilst work fell steadily behind. After a couple of centuries, the surrounding ditch could take no more bodies, and the supply of deputy project managers ran out. The results have puzzled archaeologists ever since.

ICM have issued simple guidelines for ensuring the failure of meetings. Most managers need no help in this. However, in case Buckden should prove difficult, I give below one or two of the most useful:

- Invite as many people as possible.
- Never issue an agenda.
- Deal with as much as possible (especially if it is already on the agenda) under 'matters arising'.
- As Chair, and especially if you are the boss, begin the discussion by stating your views dogmatically.
- If important issues are to be discussed, place them towards the end of the agenda. If possible, deal with them just after a heavy, alcohol-laced meal.
- Ensure that the less important the item the longer is spent discussing it.

Noise can be a great help in destroying meetings. You can usually arrange for the central heating boiler to be decoked, the road outside torn up or a car alarm to go off. By combining this with stifling heat, so that closed windows ensure near suffocation, any meeting can be reduced to impotence and its members to gibbering idiocy.

Distractions are useful. Just as the conversation at the next table in a restaurant is more interesting than our own, so what goes on outside the window or in the next office will command more attention than what is being said inside a meeting.

The telephone

You will have heard of Groton. As you know, he made misuse of the telephone his own. I mentioned some of the problems he has created with mobile phones in my first letter. Just a sample or two here, therefore, of his other advice in what he calls, in an old-fashioned phrase, 'telephone-one-upmanship'. You must find ways of teaching your victim to:

- Answer the phone either the second it rings (for maximum surprise), or after the longest possible delay (for impatience and ill-feeling). Choosing either approach at random will have the added advantage of puzzling regular callers.
- Bark out his surname, rapidly and incomprehensibly. This will wrong-foot callers, who will be in doubt as to what he said and either carry on hoping they have the right person or risk angering him by asking for a repetition. If asked to repeat his name, he should imply that anyone who does not at once recognize it is an imbecile.
- Not respond at once to whatever is said. This will make the caller unsure if the line is dead or he is.
- Select a voice and manner that complements that of the caller. Thus a hesitant caller should be replied to in a hectoring and impatient tone, an angry caller in an unresponsive, stupid voice, and a friendly and positive caller in a peculiar and incomprehensible regional accent.
- Make occasional, odd and unexplained noises; chewing, clicking, placing the hand over the mouthpiece, etc. These will puzzle callers and throw them off their stride.
- In concluding a call, always get the caller's name wrong.

Machinery

Buttercrambe encouraged the use of the word 'communications' to suggest what humans now call 'hardware' – telephones, radio, faxes, television and computer networks. This is great fun – you will remember what I told you about toys in my last letter.

Of course, we have to admit that some of these can be of value, some of the time, in effective management. But this is rare. When you have time, look through their cupboards and filing cabinets and start a collection of discarded and unused frippery, every item of which was once, if only for a couple of days, a source of childish excitement and pride of ownership.

On the other side of the coin, Buttercrambe has persuaded some managers to see the use of hardware, especially a typewriter-style keyboard, as beneath their dignity. He has obfuscated the advantages in efficiency that direct production of their own memos, letters and reports ensures. With his delicious sense of humour, he even arranged an alternative for these status-conscious individuals in the form of a 'mouse' with which they could play. To be fair, not many do.

Telepathy

As all members of the Lowerarchy are telepathic, you will not need me to write what I wish to say on this subject; tune into MDU 376.

Make more use of Srebmun. But remember he has been dormant for many years, and will need your guidance. Take care in using The Curate; remember the ambivalence of his position.

Barripper

Garden Flat
Bristol
Friday 14 February

Dear Michael

This time it's communication that I want to discuss with you, but Isuspect that comes as no surprise; yet again, your letter arrived with uncanny timing. I wish I'd paid more attention to it.

Last Tuesday, I received a call from Mr Hines. It was the first time he had acknowledged my presence since I arrived. The discussion was brief but as far as I could make out, he wanted me to undertake a major review of the company's resources. He did not make clear which resources. At one stage, he was using the word 'costs'. The only thing I felt clear about was that he wanted me to get on with it at once.

I decided to call a meeting of senior staff, and sent a memo to my colleagues straight away:

MEMO

From   *Andrew Buckden (Projects)*

To   *Sue Archer (Marketing)*
                Alan Bowden (Finance)
                Arthur Harris (Admin)
                Jim Peterson (Production)

Re   *COSTS AND RESOURCES*

Please attend a meeting in the old Board Room on Thursday 2 January at 10.30 to discuss costs and the use of resources. I expect everyone to come forearmed with all the information requisite for full discussion.

Andrew Buckden.

Unfortunately, it turned out 2 January was a Monday, not a Thursday, and we were already into February, which was what I intended to say anyhow, so Joan got a string of calls asking what I meant.

Looking at the memo again I decided I could have made it more explicit but I thought it would only make things worse if I tried to sort them out at this stage.

At 10.30 on Monday 2, I was sitting, alone, in the old Board Room. It is a room large enough to seat fifty people. I felt lonely, and wondered if everyone had decided I'd meant Thursday after all. Or

perhaps I'd got the wrong room; it was certainly too large for the number of people who were due to come. I was gazing out of the window wondering whether to give up when they started to trickle in. At 10.45 Joan arrived with a flipchart followed by another secretary struggling with an overhead projector. To say I felt guilty was an understatement.

I called everyone to gather at my end of the room. No one was keen to move, let alone sit in the front row. However, in the end we reorganized the chairs. It was only when I turned on the OHP that I realized there was no screen. I decided this time I would get it myself. Ten minutes later, I started again.

'Good morning,' I began importantly. 'You all know why we are here.'

It wasn't my fault that, just as I opened my mouth, a noise like a motorbike warming up came from the corridor. It was a pneumatic drill. I wasn't sure what to do for the best, but struggled on.

'. . . I would now like to ask for suggestions.'

The look on several faces told me that I was about to get one or two fairly pointed ones. However, apart from the drill, which seemed to be getting louder, there was total silence. After a long gap, things started to happen.

Jim: 'I have said it for two years or more – if I can't have new machinery then I need more people. Unless I can recruit another five qualified machinists before the summer, there's no way I can cover for annual leave. And if the night–shift is to remain productive, I need at least four more experienced fitters.'

The drill stopped. The silence was deafening.

Me: 'That reminds me. Mr Hines asked me to find out when he will get your proposals for equipment replacement? He said he asked you for them about nine months ago.'

Jim: 'I've made a number of proposals on new machinery., They've all been ignored in the past. I'm working on it this time with Roland. He is in contact with the manufacturers. Shouldn't Roland be here?'

Me: OK. So when can I tell Mr Hines to expect your recommendations?'

Jim: 'That's with Roland at the moment, as I explained.'

Me: 'But I have to report to Hines.'

Jim: 'I'll tell Roland to contact you.'

Jim looked tired. I knew I had been clumsy, and guessed that he would take no further part in the meeting. He was twitching with his bleeper, expecting, no doubt another machine breakdown to call him away.

The drill started again. Why on earth couldn't they stop for half an hour? I tried to get things moving again.

Me: 'Sue, could we cut staff if we focused our marketing on a smaller number of product lines? Have you thought about that?'

Sue: 'This is a critical time. The market is diversifying rather than condensing. If we withdraw from any more market sectors now it will have major repercussions.'

Me: 'But surely the range of Blue Garden Gnomes is redundant? Hines told me he'd expected to see that go in my first week here.'

Sue: 'That's our best cash cow right now. I've bought some projections along to show which products we ought to be concentrating on.'

I groaned – quietly – as she distributed a wad of papers. At least it would make a change from listening to the drill. She continued.

Sue: 'I think that if we are here to discuss reductions in expenditure then we should begin by understanding why, and then taking a rational look at the business plan and where we are failing to meet it.'

I was stumped by this. The drill was beginning to drive me crazy. Then Arthur rounded on me.

Arthur:'Andrew, what have to got to say? Sue's making a fair point, and it was you who called the meeting.'

I saw a vindictive gleam in his eyes, and knew I was in trouble, but Heaven was on my side. Even as his mouth opened, his mobile phone rang and with a brief apology he left the room. Then Hines' secretary popped her head round the door and asked Sue to go up to see him. I took the chance to tell Alan and Jim that the meeting was closed. I helped Joan cart off the unwanted overhead and flip chart; the pneumatic drill stopped as we trickled by.

Two days later I received a memo from Hines asking me to obtain and collate proposals from my colleagues on improving the utilization of all our resources as quickly as possible. I think it a strange way to delegate work, but each day seems to bring something strange, and my doubts about him grow.

I had lunch with Alan hoping to pick his brains on Hines' way of doing things. He had no answers to my questions. In fact I think he quietly shared many of my views.

Back in my office, my diary reminded me to get on with my memo to the regional managers about the forthcoming Open Day. For the 23rd I'd written 'Sue – Mr Smunch – Poland.' Now what on earth was that? I can't even communicate with myself now.

Having re-read your letter and checklist, I realize that I have made just about every mistake in the book. But at least I know how to start getting my communication better.

Yours gratefully

Andrew

Extract from letter from Michael to Andrew dated 8 February

. . . To repeat what I've told you in the past, it's the simple things that go wrong. Often enough there's nothing wrong with communication systems, but it's the communicators who fail. It is they who let their colleagues, their organization and themselves down. Again there are simple checkpoints, too often forgotten or ignored:

- It's easy to say that it's someone else's fault if you are not clear on what you are doing. Check for clarification; insist on it, and place as much importance on listening and understanding as on giving communication.
- Body language is interesting but do not let it become an obsession. Be aware of posture, nuance and inflection as they can provide valuable, unspoken clues. Do not misinterpret them for hard facts. It's just as important to shown that you are listening; most speakers can sense when you aren't.
- Choose meeting rooms with care to avoid interruptions and distraction. Check out rooms in advance and ensure that they are equipped with what you need.
- The basic rules for successful meetings are relatively straightforward – that is probably why they are seldom followed:

  - Distribute papers and agenda in advance.
  - Clarify the reasons for the meeting, and its finishing time, to everyone.
  - Get the right people there, arrive on time and manage the time.
  - Do the hard thing and exclude all those with nothing to contribute.

- When writing, use simple words and short sentences. Never pad letters or reports. Keep them concise with the fewest possible words to convey your meaning accurately. Put yourself in the position of the reader and aim to express yourself, not impress him or her. Even a simple memo for a meeting can cause problems if you are not clear on what you want to say.
- Your telephone manner is crucial as it often provides the only picture people have of you. I'll return to this another time.
- As a final point, remember what I said about planning in my last

letter and do not be too hasty to jump in at the deep end. There are always pitfalls to avoid, and dangers will emerge from unexpected quarters.

THOU SHALT BOTH GIVE AND RECEIVE COMMUNICATION EFFECTIVELY

Michael

The Fourth Letters – Customer Service

Dear Relubbus

At last the news I have from you is encouraging. The description of Buckden's meeting was a joy to read. Keep this up! However, he seems to have found a source of help which may thwart our efforts. Find out who this is and report to me urgently.

In the meantime, I would draw your attention to Buckden's colleague Archer; I am informed that he has been working closely with her in recent weeks. The sexual dimension will always remain the tempter's strongest suit; you should set yourself the objective of turning a positive and harmless relationship into the undoing of both.

However, to your next lesson. Whatever else they do or do not do, earthly managers must serve their customers. From the outpouring of publications, a tempter who was not fully indoctrinated might conclude that customers were now well served on earth. This would be an error. The truth is that Customer Service has become a field rich with pickings for consultants, writers and trainers. All of these have a vested interest in it so remaining and, you may rest assured, many of them are either double agents or fully in our pay.

I have been studying Buckden's tapes (something I am sure you spend much time doing yourself), and have found a weakness which I look to you to exploit: at an office party last Christmas he was heard to say to a junior secretary: 'Thank goodness I don't have customers to pester me.'

If Buckden worked within the public sector, this would, of course, merit his immediate promotion. Luckily for us he is in a supposedly profit-making organization, and this statement (which you can check on Tape MT/AB/91/0234 at minute 45.12) should, with due attention on your part, be enough to bring him firmly within our grasp.

Most managers will, when asked who their customers are, give the wrong answer. Some may give a vague definition of their organization's customer, although many cannot. Try asking 'civil servants' who their customers are, or local government officers, members of the armed forces, teachers, or, for a real belly laugh, the prison service or the police.

But, in fact, very few managers know who their customers are. From Buckden's remark, it is certain he cannot. As he so lucidly stated, he has no contact with his organization's customers. However, he has failed to realize that his customers are the colleagues and other internal departments he serves. If, as he claimed, he had no customers, there would be no reason for his existence. This is a situation we will arrange for him in due course, but not yet. For the moment, you must keep him in his state of ignorance.

There are Eight Golden Rules for Customer Neglect. They are best remembered by the checklist devised by Flasby, an ex Master of ICM (whose subsequent career was an unhappy one, but this is irrelevant). The Rules are:

- Know best what customers want
- Never be polite
- Install bureaucratic procedures
- Communicate as little as possible
- Keep your own customer–contact staff down
- Equivocate about delivery
- Refuse after sales service and support
- Say 'no' to all complaints

I will now outline the working of each of the Flasby principles.

Know best what customers want

The motto was best stated by one of ICM's most famous Alumni – Henry Ford: 'They can have any colour car they want, as long as it's black.' We inspired Ford to establish the principle whilst he was also wrecking the lives of those who worked for him on his 'production line' The invention of the production line is a great triumph, for which I accept some small credit. It thrives still, despite pernicious devices such as 'self-determining work groups', 'quality circles' and similar sick-making nonsense. Let those amongst our number tremble whose negligence allowed such things to grow; their fate will be dire indeed when their cover is blown. However, I digress. Ford's other principle – that the customer must like what the supplier wants to supply – has been, in the long term, equally pernicious.

To this day, cars are sold not on features that customers want, but that their makers believe they should, such as top speeds twice the legal limit and sun roofs in countries where the sun rarely shines. The computer industry thrives on producing expensive answers to questions no one has asked. Public transport organizations run trains, buses and flights at times that suit them rather than their customers.

Never be polite

Buckden's tapes show that he already follows the second rule of customer neglect – he sees customers as a nuisance. A BR guard was recently heard to remark: 'Passengers are the cause of all the trouble; this railway would run much better without them.' An hour in the Outpatients Department of one of our approved list of hospitals, doctor's surgeries, libraries, local authority housing departments or unemployment benefit offices will show you the skills required.

Install bureaucratic procedures

If, despite our best efforts, customers still wish to order something, all is not lost. With good tradecraft it is possible to make life so painful that they quickly abandon all hope.

This is a skill which we have taught to public authorities worldwide with unparalleled success. Customers are faced with insolent, incomprehensible forms which ensure that the services are used as little as possible. The Commission of the European Community has carried this art-form to its highest pinnacle yet, with paperwork so complex that an industry has grown up specializing in its interpretation. This is generally accepted as Flasby's finest work. His successor is attempting to popularize procedures for interpretation of the interpretation. My feeling is that he has gone too far.

Communicate as little as possible

Flasby called this his 'mushroom' factor; customers should be kept in the dark and showered at intervals with organic manure. Accurate information must be withheld from them and unintelligible rubbish substituted at every stage.

Here again, our greatest successes have been with public transport providers. We have succeeded in persuading them that time and fare tables at bus stops and stations are unnecessary. If provided, Flasby has shown, it is cheaper to leave indefinitely than replace with each new issue. The incomprehensibility of his timetable formats is celebrated. His list of suggested footnotes runs to 231 entries (e.g. 'SQS, stops by request only on every other Sunday before 31 September'). But it was Flasby's genius to demonstrate that timetables could be supplemented by avalanches of detailed amendments before issue.

The display of misleading destination indicators on buses and trains, whilst still popular in some areas, is now regarded as rather *passé*.

Computer and software manufacturers score a close second. We have persuaded both hardware and software manufacturers to create products so complex, and describe them in language so unfathomable, that many customers abandon them unused. More recently, we have encouraged suppliers to provide 'helplines'. Some have installed telephones that are permanently engaged; others refuse information to customers who will not pay extra for answers to the problems their incompetence has created.

Keep your own customer-contact staff down

Managers who see their customers as the lowest form of life will naturally see those whose job is to deal with them in the same light. They will pay them little, give them no training, offer them no opportunities for promotion, blame them for every complaint, and keep them at the bottom of the heap. With this background, first-rate customer neglect is assured.

In particular, we have taught managers that telephonists and receptionists are junior staff, and must be paid and treated accordingly. My Watchers report that Buckden treats such members of his organization with respect. See this does not continue; show him the patronizing jocularity used by most of his colleagues.

Equivocate about delivery

Salespeople can invariably be persuaded to promise features, prices and delivery that cannot be achieved. Most sectors score well in this area. An armoury of excellent reasons has been developed for not supplying their products on time and having no idea when they will be supplied. Many of these reasons are equally applicable to letters and payments. As ever, we have had the clearest success with public transport operators, especially air and rail carriers. They start by refusing information about delays or problems. If something must be said, they produce meaningless drivel boomed out by incomprehensible tannoys.

Our other prize pupils are the medical world. They manage to add insult to injury, as a patient (the word is significant) foolhardy enough to ask a receptionist how long he will be kept waiting for an overdue appointment quickly finds out.

ICM runs an annual competition for the best excuses for delayed delivery. Recent entries include:

- 'The computer is down.'
- 'We've had an outbreak of whooping cough at the warehouse.'
- 'The sales director went on holiday with the keys.'
- 'We sent them to your old address.'
- 'Our driver got no reply so he brought them back.'
- 'We're not allowed to deliver during Ramadan.'
- 'We understood you would contact us when you were ready for them.'
- 'We've got someone new on the switchboard.'
- 'It was the wrong type of snow.'

Refuse after-sales service and support

'After-sales service' is another fruitful field for customer neglect. We have persuaded many managers that customers can be exploited at this stage with impunity, because they are 'captive'.

Put a few of these suggestions to Buckden as opportunity allows:

- Build in maximum obsolescence, so that parts and replacements become impossible to obtain.
- Aim to make most profit from those who have committed themselves to you, by charging grossly exaggerated prices for spare parts, maintenance and consumables.
- Ensure that service parts and consumables are only obtainable after substantial delay.
- Should the customers have problems using your product, get your people to make them feel small and stupid when they seek advice.

A recent ploy is to suggest that managers should supply after-sales service and support only to those who take out expensive 'service agreements'. We are winning hands-down in this area.

Say 'no' to all complaints

Complaints are the most fertile ground of all on which to base customer neglect. Most people see complaints as a threat, an insult and a nuisance.

As Buckden is proud and quick-tempered, there is every hope that he can be taught to resent complaints. The real key is to ensure that he continues to feel insecure in his new role; insecure individuals are unable to take what they see as criticism. You should also persuade him that it is his duty to protect his staff against criticism, and thus reject all complaints against them.

I am sure you will find many other ways of ensuring the comprehensive neglect of Buckden's customers.

Your uncle

Barripper

Garden Flat
Bristol
Saturday 7 March

Dear Michael

Thank you for your last letter and guidance. I'm beginning to expect it from you, and the unbelievable appropriateness it has to my current problems. Is it some kind of self-fulfilling prophecy, or can you really see into my future?

As your checklist implies, my current problems centre round customers. Let me give you the latest chapter of my saga.

About a week ago I was trying to get down to some constructive thinking on cost savings when my phone rang. I grabbed it and barked my name in what I am prepared to believe was not the friendliest of voices. The caller said 'Sorry wrong number' and was hanging up when I recognized Sue's voice and apologized.

'Just as well I wasn't a customer,' she said. 'I'm just ringing to confirm Mr Smyrnzc's visit next week.'

'Who?'

Sue explained patiently that Mr Smyrnzc was from the Warsaw Trade Delegation.

'From the what?' My responses forced her to remind me, still with remarkable patience, that she had rung about two weeks ago, asking me to host a visitor from Poland.

Then it clicked; this was the 'Mr Smunch' in my diary.

'Look Sue, can I pass on this one? Mr Hines has dumped a pile of urgent work on me. Can't you find someone else?'

'It's too late to find someone else. Two weeks ago you said you'd be happy to look after him.'

That was two weeks ago.

'When is it then?'

I knew I was behaving like a Neanderthal, but this was all I needed – two lost days showing operations and procedures to a man from Poland with a name like a chocolate bar.

Having reluctantly agreed to look after him, I dismissed the matter from my mind, and tried to get Roland Brown on the phone to arrange to see him about my resources project. I hadn't invited him to my disastrous meeting; perhaps it was just as well. After about fifteen rings, he came through:

'Yes?' he said fiercely.

'Roland?' I asked. 'Andrew Buckden here.'

A deep silence at the other end.

'Roland, Mr Hines has asked me to look at possibilities for improving our use of resources. Can you spare a few minutes to talk it over?'

'I'm tied up.'

'Of course. I didn't mean now this minute. When would be a good time for you?'

'I've a lot on. Have a word with my assistant.'

'I really wanted your input on this. Hines thinks it's important.'

I heard the phone go down.

Whilst I was brooding about this, Sue came in. I was glad she'd come. We'd struck up a good relationship since our first encounter and now I felt I'd made a mess of it on the phone. I wanted to apologize; perhaps more important, I needed her help on this resource business.

She had hardly begun when the phone rang. For a fleeting moment, I thought it might be a contrite and helpful Roland. Of course it was no such thing.

'This latest consignment of garden gnomes. Thirty of them are useless. What are you going to do about it?'

'You must have the wrong extension. I'll put you back to the switchboard.'

'I've had a bellyful of your switchboard and unhelpful people. I've already been transferred three times this morning. The first individual couldn't understand English, the second was too busy, and the third was even ruder than you. So, my friend, what are to going to do about my gnomes?'

Sue was pricking up her ears.

'You need to speak to the Sales Department. I understand they have a complaints form.'

The telephone exploded.

'Well, as I have tried to explain, it isn't actually my responsibility. However, I will have a word with Sales as soon as I can.'

'How soon is soon?'

'I will do what I can.'

'And your name, my friend?'

I contemplated telling him it was none of his business, but reluctantly admitted what I was called. The phone went dead at once.

Sue looked concerned but she covered my embarrassment for the second time that morning as she explained that she'd finally got the go-ahead to spend extra cash on a new customer service programme which she had proposed some time ago. Apparently, Mr Hines' refusal to spend any money had been attacked by Sales and Marketing. There had been arguments and shouting behind closed doors and when Sue had been called away from my meeting she had told Hines in no uncertain terms that he was incapable of looking to the future. In the end Mr Hines had snatched victory from the jaws of defeat by letting it be known that the idea had been his in the first place.

The problem was that the Sales Department had been sitting on customer information for years without doing anything with it. They had never analysed complaints. I was listening to her but at the back of my mind, that last telephone call was still preying on my mind.

Sue went on: 'Customers are central to everything we do. If we haven't got that right, then we are all wasting our time.'

'That reminds me, Sue. That unpleasant individual on the phone when you came in was complaining about some faulty gnomes. I explained that it wasn't my job, but he insisted on telling me.'

'Who was he?'

I stopped breathing for several seconds.

'As a matter of fact, I didn't ask him. He slammed the phone down before I could. Sorry about that.'

Sue seemed to take the matter to heart more than I had expected.

First thing the next morning, I phoned Roland again, but there was no reply. I was annoyed; there should be better ways than this for contacting people. At that moment the phone rang. It was the MD's secretary, with a summons to the MD's Office. I was surprised, but walked along the carpeted corridor with a clear conscience. However, the expression on Lady Grazier's face as I was announced was not reassuring.

'Ah, Mr Buckden. Perhaps you are able to explain why a dissatisfied customer should ring me direct and leave me your name.'

The remainder of the interview was one of the more painful experiences of my life. She made no attempt to rub my face in the dirt, and did not threaten me.

'You're new; I'll make a bargain with you. Sort the problem out;

don't make the same mistake again, and the matter ends there. Agreed?'

'Agreed.' I said humbly.

I spent the rest of the morning tracing the identity of the customer. I rang him up and arranged to call on him that afternoon, equipped with authority to make whatever settlement I judged appropriate.

I had planned to have a bite with Sue at lunchtime; I felt the need for a sympathetic ear and a friendly smile. We went out to the Dog and Duck, which was usually quiet, although as it happened, Arthur was there with a friend that day. We waved at him, and sat at a table at the opposite end of the bar.

Talking to Sue made me realize what an idiot I'd been. She had been looking at the complaints log and concluded that we took the complaint merely to placate customers; we never listened to what they had to say. Sue's recommendations included scrapping the Complaints Department and creating a new Customer Care Centre whose objective was to serve customers, not shield the organization.

That was when the penny dropped. I realized that I'd been acting the same way as Complaints had been treating customers. Roland and Arthur were guilty too. Their typical responses: 'I'm too busy', 'not enough time', 'I can't get to that just yet' were all part of the same lazy approach. Roland's curt manner on the telephone had annoyed me but now I realized that I was just as bad. I remembered with embarrassment how I tried to worm my way out of hosting Mr Smunch. I cringed as I thought of my response on the telephone to the man with the useless gnomes.

The meeting with Ronald Kettlewell that afternoon was another eye-opener. He ran a large garden centre a few miles from United Group. I found him unloading a consignment of shrubs.

He continued working while we spoke.

'Brought my gnomes, have you?'

'Yes, they're in the truck. I'm sorry about the misunderstanding yesterday.'

'See this lot, lad?' He waved a hand expansively around the

centre, which was packed with people. 'Customers, they are. The people who pay my wages. If they don't like what I do, what do you think they do?'

'Go somewhere else.'

'Got it in one. So what d'you think I do?'

'Give them what they want.'

I turned to go. 'Still got your job, have you?' he asked, with a not unkindly wink.

Mr Hines' absence of any guidance is beginning to concern me a little. I'm picking up plenty to do but I read through my job description again – it's beginning to seem meaningless.

I wonder what problems you will anticipate for me next.

My thanks and best wishes

Andrew

Extract of letter from Michael to Andrew dated 1 March

. . . knowing what your customers want helps you to identify future customers. In that way they are not only an end but the means to that end. Not using your customers as a resource is tantamount to neglect of their goodwill. If they don't bear you any goodwill then you won't be in business for long. To summarize:

- Focus on what your customers want, not on what you want to give them. Remember that every manager has internal customers, and find out who yours are. Find out what your colleagues do and how you can help them.
- Treat your customers and colleagues with the respect and courtesy you expect from others. Remember that you are all part of a larger team and that you must work with them again tomorrow, and the next day. Think of the needs of those who have more direct customer contact than yourself, the Marketing

manager, Sue Archer, for example. You will need her help as much as she seems to need yours.

- Don't promise nothing if providing a service is what you are there for. On the other hand don't promise people the earth if you can't deliver it.
- Never say 'it's not my department' to a customer; it is not the customer's problem to sort it out, but yours and remember that you want them to come back in the future.
- Develop a good telephone voice and manner. Seven times out of ten this is where business, and friendships, come to grief. Don't be offhand when you answer a call; if you are preoccupied with other things, then make arrangements for calls to be picked up elsewhere.
- Don't be aggressive when people pressure you, and never make a customer feel foolish.
- Regard complaints as opportunities. Often the dissatisfied customer will become loyal in the future if you take time to understand the problem and take action to put it right.
- If you are not serving customers, your job is to serve someone who is.

> THOU SHALT KNOW AND SEEK TO SATISFY
> THY MARKET

Michael

The Fifth Letters –
Using Resources

Dear Relubbus

I note another minor success in your hitherto feeble attempts to drag Buckden down to perdition. Redirecting that complaint to Buckden and involving the MD reminded me of one or two escapades from my own time as a junior tempter, although the final result was equally unsatisfactory. More to the point were the seeds you have sown in regard to the Archer woman. This is consoling news for your long-suffering Uncle – keep up the bad work!

You have arranged for Buckden to be directed towards the use of resources. From now on, we must make this theme central to all our efforts. Your basic training will have taught you that earthly managers are expected to 'use all their resources to best advantage'. Few of them know what their resources are, let alone how to use them. Ensure that Buckden's confusion on these points remains complete. Research by Rhosllanerchrugog has shown that the most useful resources for causing problems are:

- The market
- Human resources
- Reputation
- Information
- Finance
- Time

and I recommend you to learn how to use these before attempting to exploit others.

The market

Unless there is a market, there is no reason to employ any resources at all, including managers. Marketing managers usually understand this; over the years we have blinded other managers to it. Most have never defined the market for their operation, let alone asked whether they are using it to the best advantage. The fact that the market is, in most cases, internal to their organization, makes not a jot of difference. Or rather, it should make no difference. However, as managers share the same blindness, they do not challenge each other. Besides, it would be considered impolite.

Some years ago practitioners of a technique with the pompous title of 'organization and methods (O & M)' went around asking awkward questions such as 'Why?' and 'Why not?' The position looked dangerous for a time, but we need not have worried. Humans recoil from such questions, and managers soon relegated O & M practitioners to standing around with clipboards and stop watches observing typists, or adding up microseconds to find out how long it should take a messenger carrying the morning's mail to mount to the tenth floor. Organization and Methods sank without trace some years ago.

Human resources

This is the resource that offers the best chance of leading managers astray.

Managers used to refer to their subordinates as 'hands', a view still taken by many of them – uniform, unthinking, unintelligent units of labour. A clever piece of work by a double agent called McGregor encapsulated this view in his 'Theory X'.

Theory X gave respectability to the instinctive beliefs of generations of managers. Most humans are (I am ashamed to admit) motivated by the urge to contribute to the work of their organization

and their community, to succeed and to be seen by others as successful, and to grow and become better people. But, as a race, managers are convinced that their subordinates are motivated exclusively by money, and are lazy, dishonest, stupid and untrustworthy. Encourage Buckden to believe Theory X; it is easier than you may think.

McGregor's ambiguous description of a 'Theory Y' has caused us a good deal of difficulty. Despite your efforts. Buckden may start to realize that those working for him have similar motivation to his own. But he must never be allowed to see them as human beings with the same potential to provide a resource of knowledge, skill, helpfulness, commitment, good humour and creativity. As long as he believes he is different from and better than those who work for him, he will ultimately be ours.

I will return to the misuse of the human resource in a later letter.

Reputation

The reputation, 'goodwill', or image of an organization is a specialized matter. Several decades of inspired work by the MDU have ensured that many organizations now regard their image as more important that their product. We have even started to apply the PR (PR = Perpetual Racket) concept to the so-called democratic processes. The results have been outstanding; already, no political party can consider fighting an election without PR help. There are rumours that our next assignment will be the public image of the All Lowest Himself.

Information

'If I tell you all I know, you'll be as wise as me.' This axiom was enunciated by Clovenfield over three aeons ago: knowledge is power on earth as it is with us. Managers have always been regarded, by themselves at least, as the founts of all wisdom and an admission of ignorance has been unthinkable. By keeping their knowledge a close secret, they have tried to maintain their supposed superiority.

Successful management now depends on the efficient acquisition, storage and exchange of information. Unless we can prevent it, this revolution will change managers' attitude to knowledge of all kinds. It may also change as they realize they can no longer acquire a stock of knowledge that will last them through their whole career; skill obsolescence stares them in the face. Our task, therefore, is to maintain the illusions of the past.

Today, more and more information is held by machine. Buttercrambe's greatest achievement during the 60s and 70s was to relieve managers of millions of pounds in return for whirring disk drives and flashing computers that spewed out thousands of pages of unwanted and incomprehensible printouts to clutter their offices and fill their filing cabinets. It is here, not on the occasional letter or report, that the forests have really gone.

Buttercrambe was demoted to Board level for these achievements, but I have to say that his successors have not shown the same inspiration. However, IOMT is now fighting back. It has increased the pace of change, so that no one can settle down. It has strengthened the failing arms of computer managers in their attempts to retain control over their empires. It has played on manager's desire to 'keep up with the Joneses' and use 'state-of-the-art technology'. It has invented the computer virus.

Above all, IOMT has welded the concept of 'information technology' and electronics together. Managers no longer see pen and paper, pocket-books, card indices, diaries, calendars or the other hundred-and-one cheap and effective methods of information storage and retrieval as 'IT'. The up-to-date manager would not be seen dead using them.

Finance

This is the sphere in which the power of jargon as a weapon of misinformation has been most clearly demonstrated. Thanks to Clovenfield and his brilliant team of ex-accountants the simple facts about money have been so fogged that few managers trust themselves to understand them, and those that do mostly get it wrong.

A few years ago, Clovenfield arranged for the majority of Board-level posts to be filled by accountants. This was a great ploy. Designers, engineers, salespeople, production personnel and the rest were so successfully squeezed under the thumbs of the accountants that many organizations died from slow strangulation of ideas, creativity and risk-taking. He also arranged for accountants to award themselves the title of 'controller' (or the even more pompous 'comptroller') to emphasize their supreme regard for themselves.

Some members of the Lowerarchy were a little concerned, a decade or two ago, when Clovenfield suggested that the time had come for managers to be given courses in 'Management Accounting for Non-Financial Managers', but they failed to appreciate his subtlety. The suggestion was brilliant; almost without exception, those attending such courses have left them more convinced than ever that accountancy is a closed world into which it is disaster to trespass.

Clovenfield's team has produced a manual of Accountspeak, which you must master in its entirety. Here are one or two samples of its wisdom:

Depreciation

This is an ideal area. Tempters should begin by causing doubt about the method of calculation; 'Should we use the Straight Line Method, or would the Sinking Fund be more appropriate? Then again, maybe the Replacement Cost approach would show a truer picture?' After some time agonizing over this, preferably with the Company Accountant present to confuse managers even more, attention should be switched to the actual meaning of the calculation: 'Does depreciation represent real money? If so can it be used for buying new assets and if not, where have the sums actually gone?' With luck, managers will start losing sleep, and rise from their bed in the small hours to do frantic calculations on scraps of paper. Marital and partnership problems should follow.

Provisions and appropriations

'Provisions and appropriations' are of no significance whatever, but typify the Disneyland built by accountants to hedge themselves from the real world; they are the true language of Accountspeak. Managers should be regularly fed with absorption costing, accruals, contingent liabilities, marginal costs, discounted cash flow, floating charges, deployment of funds, gearing ratios, incremental costing, solvency ratio, payback periods, scrip issues and gross redemption yield, and persuaded that an understanding of all is essential to their job.

Budgetary control

This area is dangerous. Budgetary control can be an effective aid to management. The strategy is to ensure that the volume of paperwork involved is extremely large, and its completion immensely time-consuming. The setting of budgetary targets must be presented as a fight to the death between colleagues, in which, to stand a chance of winning, all must make the most outrageous demands. If, towards the end of the financial year, managers have underspent, they must be inveigled into the most extravagant, unnecessary and uncontrolled orgy of spending.

Time

Humans do not experience time as we do, and the difference is crucial to the destruction of management careers. I will try to explain.

For them, time can only pass (with a few unimportant exceptions) at an unalterable, steady speed. Thus events which occur too quickly or too slowly are difficult – even impossible – for them to perceive. This has serious effects for managers, who fail to notice slow events in particular. Many slow changes in the market-place, deteriorations in performance or in the financial position of their organization, can pass them by with disastrous results.

Strange as it may seem, humans are unable to move about in time, except in their dreams and imagination. This has several consequences: they can only experience events in an inescapable succession; they forget events that occurred in the 'past', and cannot revisit them, either to alter them or check them; they can only guess what will happen in the 'future'. Because of their problems in trying to remember and trying to foresee, some find their awareness of the 'present' – the only point in the succession in which they can act – is undermined. This effect can be particularly pronounced in managers.

Many live exclusively in the past. These can be recognized by their never-ending demands for reports: daily, weekly, monthly, annual, sales, production, accident or incident. They spend most of their time reading history, and force their subordinates to spend most of their time writing it. Most such managers work in the public sector; others who attempted to do so would rapidly find themselves writing a report on how their organization went out of business.

The largest group of managers exist exclusively in the present. They live from one unforeseen crisis to another, forever 'fire-fighting'. The in-tray, the telephone, the never-ending meetings, problems and emergencies prevent them from learning from past mistakes or planning for future success. I've noted Buckden's Production colleague, Peterson, as someone who could be useful to us in this area.

A smaller but interesting group is obsessed with what is to come. Neurotic and insecure, they devote themselves to precautions and plans against every conceivable kind of emergency. It is possible to twist the thinking of some that they become so paralysed for fear of what might happen – whether fire, bankruptcy or earthquake – that they cease to operate normally. From the reports of the Watchers, I do not think Buckden is one of these, but it may be worth looking at his girlfriend.

Other resources

At the start of this letter I referred to the many other resources which a manager must use to best advantage. There are three golden rules to ensure this does not happen:

1   *Keep his nose to the grindstone* – If he is kept fully occupied, the chances that he will notice unused resources are slight.
2   *Tell him it is not his job* – Any resources that are not regularly used are probably in a vacuum between managers' responsibilities. Buckden must either feel afraid to trespass or get himself into a situation of conflict. Play on his impetuosity.
3   *Suggest it's too difficult* – Bringing unused resources into use often requires imagination, skills or time that are not easily available. Discouragement is usually straightforward.

There is plenty for you to work on here. I await your news.

Your uncle

Barripper

Garden Flat
Bristol
Thursday 19 March

Dear Michael

It's only looking back that I realize the value of what you said in your last letter. I wish I'd paid more attention to it. My own thoughts and actions have been so confused that I've now got problems I had not expected.

I was getting nowhere on the use of resources, but inspiration struck as I arrived last week to find Joan off sick and her in-tray stacked high with the day's unopened mail. I started thinking about letters, and everything involved in producing and sending them. It reminded me of attempts I had seen in my previous organization to reduce that particular resource consumption. Using only second class post had been one such attempt. Sadly, it met problems. The slow response, especially to customers, soon got us a bad reputation. The system limped along for a while, but it wasn't long before it was buried as impractical. One idea did occur to me now. I remember that I had been told that pencils were cheaper than ball-point pens, and as I knew Joan often used pencils, I decided to order a box, so that we could phase out pens and, if it was a success, spread the idea to the whole organization. I wrote out a purchase order for a box then and there, signed it, and got it into the system.

I had just done this, when Arthur Harris paid me an unexpected visit. He seemed edgy, almost guilty. I couldn't help wondering what had brought him into my office. To my surprise, his first words echoed my own thoughts.

'I've been thinking about this initiative of Mr Hines on saving costs,' he began. 'I'm sure there's a great deal we can do together on this one.'

He sounded ingratiating, not the Arthur I knew.

'Pooling secretaries, for example, is something I've been thinking about for a long time, only no one seems prepared to listen. I know you have the ear of our director, and I'm sure you will be thinking about the possibilities.'

Something inside my head seemed to say 'this is a good one.' I asked him to sit down, and he was obviously relieved.

'It's been done in most forward-looking organizations, and I'm sure you will know of its advantages. We abolish all these separate secretaries, each working for only one or two managers, and each with their separate office, and put them all into a central 'pool'. Resources will be much better used, as those with less work will help out those who are overloaded. It saves a lot of office space too.'

I thought for a few moments but the voice inside my head was loud and clear; 'This is a winner. Hines will love this.'

I said 'Thanks for the suggestion, Arthur. I'll certainly think about it very carefully, and if I need any help, I'll come back to you.'

He got up to leave, obviously happier.

This seemed a different Arthur from the one who had rebuffed my requests for an office move. His idea would save on several key resources; money, time and human resources for sure. A typing pool should help to break down departmental boundaries and make sharing of knowledge easier.

I spent the rest of the day working up my proposal, giving it my best. I suggested that all secretaries should be moved into a pool in one location. All in all, whilst I could not yet put a figure on it, substantial savings would be made. I wrote this up as a proposal for Hines and felt that I was making real progress at last.

I'd received a note from Sue about the forthcoming Open Day, but decided that my priority was what turned out to be another unproductive meeting with Jim. The shambles and waste in Production were, according to him, the result of chronic lack of investment for more than a decade. Jim had made no end of recommendations, he said, but all of them had been shelved. His problems were beginning to get to him, especially with whispers of new environmental regulations.

Going through my in-tray. I spotted another scribbled note from Sue telling me that Mr Smunch had cancelled at the last minute. I was annoyed at the time I'd wasted preparing for his visit. After the struggle with my conscience, I had started to look forward to Mr Smunch's visit, if only to justify myself to Sue.

By the following morning I had become tense about my proposal on the typing pool and what Hines would think of it. It was the only positive suggestion I had come up with on his cost-saving campaign. I found it difficult to concentrate on anything else, and imagined every sort of disaster.

After lunch, I received a call to go up and see Hines. As I sat down, he skimmed my memo across the table.

'An excellent report, Buckden. I'm glad to see that you are at last focusing on our real needs. I suggest that you take it away and get on with it.' He looked down towards the papers on his desk; I realized that the interview was over.

My relief must have been visible. Hines realized that I had made a significant contribution to the organization's use of its resources. I made my way back to my office, having the pleasure of bumping into Sue as I did so. I asked her to spare me a few moments.

When I had described what had happened, Sue said 'Did Hines agree with your proposals, then?'

I thought about it.

'I'm not quite sure,' I said. 'But he seemed to think they were a good idea.'

'Did he say he would back you with the directors?'

'No. He left it to me to get on with.'

'But the directors will have to support it.'

'Yes, I suppose they will. But I felt he was behind me.'

'Perhaps. But exactly what is he doing behind you? Did he tell you to consult your colleagues, Andrew?'

There was something about the way she pronounced my name which made me go blank.

'Well, I think I can cope,' I said.

'Fair enough,' she said, getting up rather quickly. 'See you around.' She closed the door quietly behind her.

With her words and your advice in mind, I decided to call a meeting. I chose the list of participants with great care, including my fellow heads of department, plus (the idea popped into my head from nowhere) Peter Plews, the union rep. I sent them an agenda, and told them when it would start and was likely to finish. I drafted a presentation and rehearsed what I would say. I wasn't going to be caught unprepared this time.

As I explained my proposal, the assembled company fell silent. I emphasized how they would improve our utilization of the major resources of people, time, information, space and money. I felt confident as I sat down.

The first question came from Peter Plews who asked if I'd canvassed the secretaries for their views. He said that he thought that most would favour the one-to-one situation.

Roland Brown didn't wait for me to reply:

'Working as they now do, the secretaries gain specialist knowledge of their area; sometimes I think they know more than their bosses. That couldn't happen if they were pooled.'

While I was searching for a convincing answer to this, Arthur chimed in.

'You say a pool will make better use of marginal time; do you not feel that the lazy secretaries will still work slowly, and the conscientious ones still do more than their share. We could lose days getting work to and from the pool, especially when there are corrections.'

Thanks very much Arthur, I thought; it was your idea, wasn't it? I nearly said something, but thought better of it.

Jim said 'Is the pool to answer the phone for us, and if so, how will they know where we are when we leave the office? We're sometimes not even sure ourselves.' This raised a chuckle.

'I'm sure you aren't, Jim,' Arthur chipped in.

Alan, who had listened carefully so far, spoke at last. 'Andrew, I hear what you are saying about better use of resources. You may be right; until I see some detailed costing I wouldn't like to express a view. But any savings will rely almost entirely on higher productivity by the secretaries; the space savings you mentioned would be difficult to put to productive use. Counterbalancing those savings will be the increased need for the internal mail service, the cost of allocating an area for the pool and making the physical change, and some loss of productivity by other staff. I'm not qualified to say but I suspect that the risk to customer service could be significant too. All in all, Andrew, I remain to be convinced.'

I looked desperately towards Sue, hoping for support, but she didn't meet my eye. There was a hush.

Peter Plews, the union rep. asked quietly, 'May I take it that the agreed procedures have been followed?'

The silence became deeper.

'Perhaps you can tell me how many redundancies this will cause,' he asked, scarcely above a whisper.

It was here that I made my worst mistake. 'You should know that the scheme has been cleared by Mr Hines,' I said.

'Is that so,' replied Peter, through clenched teeth.

By this time, I was down and out, although I tried to make the best of things:

'Thanks very much for your comments, everyone. It has been a most useful meeting for me. I have taken what you say on board, and will come back to you when I have done some more homework.' Inside I felt like a pricked balloon.

That afternoon, I received a summons from Mr Hines. I went in with a heavy heart.

'I've just had a visit from Peter Plews.' be began, very quietly.

I shrank in my chair.

'He tells me that you have claimed my authority for a scheme to pool the organization's typing facilities, which will result in substantial redundancy amongst his members. I naturally told him this was not true.'

Mr Hines went on for quite a long time, never raising his voice. 'I have a final point to make to you Mr Buckden. Your conduct has led me to think seriously about your future with us. Quite apart from this extraordinary episode, your inability to propose any cost reductions, as I told you to do some time ago, leads me to ask some fundamental questions. Indeed, I am not at this moment sure whether you have a future here. I suggest you come up with something constructive while you are still contracted to do so. But this time, I want a full report not only on what you propose to do but how you propose to do it before you start making recommendations to other staff.'

I remembered Sue's words; Hines had let me down. I had invited his comments, but he had given me neither advice nor support. Now my job, such as it was, was on the line. I left, concealing a mammoth sense of injustice.

I sought out Alan. His common sense helped me to snap out of the worst. He said that I was on the right track, but had gone about it the wrong way. Our use of resources certainly was haphazard and uncoordinated. But my naive approach had been clumsy. Most of all, I was cross with myself for not taking on board some of the advice you had offered me.

I don't think I'm going to get the chop this time, but it's a close call. I need to come up with some fresh ideas – quickly.

My apologies for this letter. I can sense in advance the tone of your reply.

Andrew

Extract of letter from Michael to Andrew dated 12 March

. . . managers often concentrate on one resource, for example money, at the expense of others, such as exploiting equipment efficiently. Keeping a balance and sense of proportion should not prove beyond your capability.

Bear the following points in mind:

- Other departments are all arms of the same body; they are your customers and you theirs.
- You will not need reminding of major resources such as money, people, equipment and information. Do not neglect other resources such as your contacts and colleagues, and their knowledge and skills. The reputation of your organization and the goodwill of your customers are too often ignored.
- Do not underestimate the power of information. Its misuse is the cause of most planning errors, especially in finance. It seems that your financial accountant has a sound grasp of this. Know the cost of resources you control as he does and be aware of the negative, as well as positive, impacts of any cost savings you propose.
- Despite what I said before, be wary of too much overt goodwill. Managers have to earn the respect and trust of their people. It is not given by right. You have to learn rapidly whom you can trust and whom among your colleagues seem more devoted to their own ends. For some, colleagues are as they should be –

resources of mutual support for the organization. For others, they appear no more than puppets to be manipulated.

- Most resources – especially people and equipment – are under-utilized. Get to know the skills and strengths of the people around you. It is crucial to maximizing the use of your most valuable resource.

- Maximizing of value and minimizing of costs may appear to conflict with each other, but not necessarily. If you want to take your colleagues along with you, make sure, in any savings you propose, that you can guarantee a continuous supply of the resource they need. It may prove a critical yardstick.

THOU SHALT STRIVE TO USE ALL THY RESOURCES WELL

Michael

The Sixth Letters – Creativity

My Dear Relubbus

I was delighted to learn of your success with Buckden's typing pool scheme. This is more like it! You have also started to make excellent use of our agents. I like the situation you are setting up with the Archer woman. For the first time, I have the feeling that it may not be long before we are able to welcome Buckden into a warm hereafter. However, I still await your report on the sources of help Buckden may be getting. Treat this as a matter of urgency.

Today, I would like to draw your attention to another area with immense possibilities for amusing mayhem; that of creative thinking.

Humans love the old and familiar, the tried and tested (with the possible exception of their partners). New scenes, people, and methods cause anxiety which can reach the level of neurosis. If they have a choice, they will reject such stresses. Managers are even more liable than real people to react like this. For most of them, the fact that something has been done in a certain way for a long time is a sufficient reason for continuing to do it. Innovation and creativity result in change, and change demands extra effort and painful adjustment.

For the greater part of human history we arranged for a structure of conformity to be underpinned by a system of temporal and spiritual punishment that ensured almost total obedience to whatever cabal held power. By restricting scientific enquiry and technological innovation, we were able to send generations to their grave in the certain conviction that those who sailed too far to the West would fall off the edge of the world, that without regular human sacrifices the crops would fail, and that sun and moon revolved round the earth.

We successfully installed cultures of this kind throughout the British Empire. Its public schools, universities, clubs, regiments and civil service were amongst the finest examples of sterile conformity ever seen. The penalties exacted of those who dared to suggest there might be better ways of thinking about or doing things made medieval torture chambers look like a holiday camp.

There are two strategies available to us in the area of management creativity. They are known in the trade as TLC – Too Little Change, (the use of this acronym for Tender Loving Care is not acceptable; this obscene concept has, of course, been categorized as a form of sexual harassment) and TMC -Too Much Change.

The first option will usually be TLC. The aim here is to create a culture in which tradition is paramount, and any suggestion that there could be better ways is regarded as treason. The view must be promulgated that any attempt at creative thinking is an implied criticism of one's colleagues. To suggest that anything is less than perfect presupposes that those who designed, operated, or sold it have failed to do their job. Anyone daring to do so must therefore be pretentious and self-opinionated.

Such behaviour is easily linked to status, age or both. If the person trying to be creative is junior, young or recently appointed it is straightforward to hint that they are presumptuous and cocky. Descriptive phrases you will find useful include:

- 'too big for his boots'
- 'so sharp he is sure to cut himself'
- 'a new broom'

If the would–be creative individual possesses high qualifications, the task will be even easier. He or she will be

- 'too clever by half'
- 'wet behind the ears'
- 'all theory, no practice'

I am not sure if a lower second class degree in the humanities ranks as a 'high qualification', but it seems to me there is sufficient scope for weakening Buckden's position.

The 'public service' was an obvious milieu for submissive compliance, and TLC took a firm root there. The boardrooms of some larger organizations have also proved a fertile field, but we were delighted and surprised when several of our more innovative tempters showed how the same culture could also be transplanted into smaller organizations.

To our horror, however, several double agents were at work. They succeeded in penetrating our network and introduced the concepts of creative thinking, innovation and change into management.

We were saved by one of our great strategic coups – the discovery of Bradnop's Theory of Diminishing Circles. Whilst idly watching a group of ex local government officials being shown the error of their ways, Bradnop happened to observe the eddies of smoke that were being formed, and it occurred to him that, however many times he had observed such a scene, the smoke never repeated the same patterns; it was in a state of perpetual change. From this, it was a simple step to apply the thinking to management; if we could not prevent change, then let there be perpetual change. The day of TMC had arrived.

The concept of TMC is applied differently from TLC. By its nature, it works best if individual managers are infected rather than a whole organization or society, as with TLC. Too Much Change is thus of great practical value to tempters.

To apply TMC, you should consider whether Buckden is a

suitable for temptations such as the 'I am the only person who has thought of this one' syndrome, or the 'Let's try it a new way' approach. Each of these is an exaggeration of an attitude which, if used in moderation, would lead to success: the secret is in their compulsive, uncontrolled application.

Get him, when asked to carry out some routine task (completing the annual budget projection, for example, or recruiting a new member of staff) to challenge the procedure, refuse to complete the accepted paperwork, and insist on calling in whichever of his colleagues (the Management Accountant, the Personnel Manager or whoever) is responsible and haranguing them at length about his views. After a few similar occasions, Buckden's popularity will have slumped to a new low, and the job will have come to a standstill. My instinct again tells me he may be a good subject for this approach.

In its most extreme form, TMC can have amusing and far-reaching effects. The MDU's Organization Taxonomy offers numerous applications, amongst which the Ultimately-Fluid Organization (UFO), or Consultant's Cure-all is the best known and most generally effective. Under this, the manager or consultant leads his clients to believe that whatever form of organization is currently in use must be changed.

Thus, if the organization is decentralized, with decision-making carried out at local level, it will be suggested that power should be brought to the centre in order to ensure uniform standards, sound discipline and the exploitation of centralized buying and marketing power. If the organization already has a strong headquarters function, it will be recommended that decision-making should be devolved to the lowest level, in order to ensure flexible response to local conditions and motivate individual managers and staff.

If the organization structure provides for spans of control for managers of five or six, with several levels, then we suggest that individuals should be 'empowered' and the structure 'delayered'. Bradnop is currently having an immense success with the powerful technique of 'downsizing'. He developed this from the Roman practice of decimation, or executing every tenth man in an army that disobeyed orders. These approaches have the effect of increasing

managers' spans of control indefinitely, thus lessening the degree of control they can exercise. We persuade them that they will improve motivation whilst reducing costs.

If the organization structure already has few layers and wide spans of control, we persuade its managers that the need is to reduce them to a manageable size – i.e. to create more levels and more middle managers. We explain that only by doing this is it possible to maintain adequate control, proper career paths and prospects of promotion. The term 'upsizing' has not yet gained general acceptance.

All this is immense fun. The game is better played by using 'consultants' than attempting to influence managers directly.

The use of words is crucial. You will have noted (I hope) the superb terms listed above. Their development and introduction is an object lesson in the power of words to control and destroy human thought processes, especially in the area of management. This theme will recur throughout your work; strive to master it, both in theory and practice.

However, because the level of literacy amongst managers (not to mention consultants) is so low, words must be supported by other means. A team at ICM has been working on what they call 'pictograms'. These are simple line drawings based on basic geometrical shapes and designed to communicate elementary concepts to those of the most limited intelligence. They are simplicity itself to devise. When you have an idle moment (which I trust is very rare) try experimenting for yourself. The first stage is to sketch out a few combinations of circles, squares and triangles. If you are short of ideas, you will find a grid of between four and nine squares (anything more complex is over the head of most managers) is ideal for any purpose. Next, pick out one or two of the most striking patterns and think of a meaning to attach to them. The meaning is of no importance whatever. Finally, think of a catchy title. In this way, you have created a new management concept.

Working with these, we have installed a number of our best agents at senior level in management institutions across the world. Many have written books, engaged in consultancy, sought conference bookings, and trained others to use their pictograms, paying a royalty for the right to do so. They have made both a reputation as a guru and a large fortune. Needless to say, the royalties are paid into the Deputy Chief Tempter's benevolent fund.

As a junior tempter, your task is so to besot your manager with the cleverness of such thinking that he applies it to everything in sight, to the annoyance of his colleagues and the ultimate destruction of his operation. Keep him away from his friend in Accounts, who shows far too much common sense for my liking.

So much for creativity in management techniques. Creativity in products and services is both harder and more important to employ.

The use of TLC in this area poses no problems. The key is 'extinguisher vision', ensuring that managers are so busy fighting fires they have no time to think about anything new. Here also, words help. If a manager thinks of himself as 'a widget maker', rather than as someone who has so far satisfied a demand by making widgets (a subtle but crucial distinction), the chances are high his trade will die with him.

People can easily be led to believe they are defending their way of life and that of their colleagues by resisting change. The application of this principle to shop-floor workers through the agency of trade unions has been one of our most famous victories. I still weep tears of joy when I see what used to be London Docks, or electric locomotives with firemen. But in this field it is conceivable that we ourselves may be suffering from a touch of TLC, and some updating of our approach may be necessary.

It is easy to trap intelligent young people into TLC. By nature, most will tend towards TMC, but with suitable manoeuvring they can be turned into powerful anti-creative agents and negative, destructive thinkers. The technique is to shower them with praise for discovering problems and difficulties with other people's ideas, and suggest that this demonstrates their cleverness and clear-sightedness. It is just possible that Buckden could be turned in this way; an experiment could do no harm.

Managers who are always open to new ideas, who search for

them actively and continually, and encourage and welcome them from others are a serious problem. Our best hope is to match them with TLC colleagues and engender as much tension and bad blood as possible between them.

You do not need to worry overmuch about artificial aids to creative thinking. 'Brainstorming' was originally developed by MDU as a method of producing an appearance of much creativity with a minimum of results. It is true that it and similar approaches may get out of hand and end up with real creativity, but they are usually only used by managers who are creative by nature, and are rarely used properly. If, however, you do sense that Buckden is getting value from this approach, persuade his colleagues and subordinates to ridicule it, gently at first, and with more bitterness the more successful it is proving. The description 'flavour-of-the-monthing' can be used for this as for many similar situations.

Have fun with this one,

Your appreciative uncle

Barripper

Garden Flat
Bristol
Monday 6 April

Dear Michael

Your letter arrived with its usual impeccable timing. I've taken a little more care to read it this time. I still break out in a sweat at the thought of that last meeting with Mr Hines.

Since my last woeful outpouring I've begun to make some progress. I have targeted three resource areas in which I am convinced there are the greatest opportunities for improvement – production equipment, use of space and people. The only thing Hines has contributed is to set a deadline. I've got two months to complete the project.

I finished my last letter with a plea for a fresh perspective on old problems. Your letter once again provided me with sound advice. I sense that creativity is one of the qualities Hines does not believe I have. As it happens, I got two very different chances to prove it last week; I leave you to judge how well I did.

I called again on Arthur, to press my case for a change of office. I decided not to mention his U-turn on the typing pool. He was no more receptive than before, but I intended to persevere; dripping water wears through the hardest rock. As I was leaving, he asked how Sue was, with what looked to me like a wink. The light was not good, and I expect I was mistaken, but I hope he is not under a misapprehension.

On my long trudge back to the East Wing, I saw a crowd of people pushing and talking outside A Shop. Something large and grey was obstructing the passage. For a moment I could not believe my eyes; the doorway was blocked by an elephant's backside.

'What on earth is it?' I asked.

'Jim's circus,' said someone.

'We're housing the London zoo,' said someone else.

'New letter-box,' added a third wag.

'Latest block-busting success,' the stream of wit continued, until Jim came up behind me, and silence fell on the group.

'Right then, back to work all,' he said.

'We can't get back,' pointed out someone.

'Try the front door,' Jim said witheringly, and the group turned and disappeared, casting backward glances at the two of us.

'What you going to do, Jim? I asked.

'What gets stuck can get unstuck,' Jim said. 'Especially now we've got your help. I'm sure that unjamming elephants is one of the first lessons they teach at business school.'

I decided to ignore the jibe. 'What on earth is it?' I asked.

'An elephant's bum,' explained Jim. 'Here, give him a poke and see if that'll shift him.'

I must have looked alarmed. He handed me a shaft of wood that was lying on the floor.

I hesitated. 'Well, if you won't, I will,' he said, and jammed the shaft into a tender part of the animal with all his force. I stood clear, awaiting the inevitable kicking and trumpeting, but none came. 'Good strong stuff we make them of, isn't it?' said Jim.

I put up the best smoke-screen I could. 'Quite a change from gnomes,' I said jauntily. 'But I don't think I'd like one in my front garden.'

'Nor me,' said Jim, 'but the garden centres love 'em. Got an order book as long as his trunk. This is our development model, but we seem to have forgotten a small detail.'

'Or rather a large one,' I said, but Jim did not laugh.

'Well,' he said, 'How are you going to solve it for us? I'm sure Mr Hines will offer the company's gold medal for this one.'

It was well and truly stuck in the doorway. Quite how it had got so firmly jammed no one seemed to know. However, that wasn't really the problem, any more than how to get it out. What mattered was to ensure that it didn't happen again, as the production line geared up to the targeted thirty elephants a day. Here was a real opportunity for creative thinking.

I walked round the Shop, studying the layout, machinery and equipment. I got the shift and other manning details from Jim's clerk. My brain was fertile that morning, and I soon had an interesting list of possibilities:

- Cutting a bigger doorway
- Producing the elephants in four parts and reassembling outside A Shop
- Transferring production to an area with a bigger doorway
- Designing an inflatable model, to be blown up when outside the door.

Jim saw further problems with all these ideas both on cost and inconvenience.

I left work that night with the problem still on my mind; I thought of it all evening and much of the night, much to Laura's displeasure. About two in the morning, I felt I had begun to devise a way forward, but by morning I'd come up with nothing that seemed worth discussing with Jim.

When I looked in at A Shop he was just finishing with another panic.

'Sorted out our elephants, have you?' he asked with a twinkle in his eye.

'Not entirely,' I said, studying his expression. 'Funny sort of shape, your doorway, isn't it?' I ruminated, staring at it sideways.

He followed my glance. Yes, the door was distinctly wider than it was high.

'You don't think . . .?' he asked.

'Might do.' I said.

'Ever taken a big table through a small door? On its side, twisting it as you go.'

Jim got two fitters to help us. In three minutes, we had Jumbo through and standing on his feet in the passage. Jim asked why I hadn't suggested it yesterday.

'Only just thought of it', I replied. I understand it takes them under a minute now.

I couldn't resist asking Sue out for lunch at the Dog and Duck to tell her the story of the elephant's bum. It is usually pretty quiet there, but this was a bad day. There was a wedding party, and the lounge was packed with people snapping off photographs and shouting at each other through their champagne. We tried to struggle through to the other bar, but it was just as bad. We gave up. Trying to get out through the door, we were crushed against each other when some fool fired off a camera at us; I suppose they thought we were guests. I certainly hope that picture doesn't see the light of day; it might be misunderstood!

Somehow the episode of the elephant's bum seemed a kind of preparation for more serious matters. I felt I had learnt a good deal about real creativity and the problems it can cause. I went back to my three target areas; equipment, space and people with a clear mind.

I followed your advice to strike up a dialogue with the people involved right at the start. I needed to include Roland from

Purchasing; he was hard to approach but I had no choice. Next was Martin Fellows, a graduate trainee who was firmly under Arthur's protective wing in Office Administration. Martin was being trained in personnel work but I'd heard that Arthur had made a strong case for his transfer to A & O. Martin hadn't been seen since. Finally, there was Jim in Production.

Roland was central to the question of resources. He had a curious attitude towards waste and could see duplication across the board but had never done anything about it. He agreed reluctantly to join the project.

Martin told me that the office reallocation scheme, which Arthur had used to red-herring me before, was no more than a paper exercise. It was obvious that Martin had a few ideas of his own, but I realized the need to keep Arthur in the picture. I had upset enough people recently.

The elephant's bum had given Jim and me a better understanding of each other. Jim was annoyed with the Directors for ignoring his past warnings and recommendations on the state of his equipment. He was actually quite pleased that someone was asking questions, but he didn't hold out much hope for improvement.

I wanted Roland, Martin and Jim to take an imaginative look at their operations in order to overcome problems instead of living with them. I needed their support if my report to Hines was going to carry weight.

I was secretly pleased that Jim and Roland turned up on time but we started on a sour note with snide comments about a new broom sweeping clean. (I'd forgotten that I'd only been at United Group for six months – it seemed like a life-time.) I challenged Roland when he accused me of wanting to build my own empire, asking whether he really thought that was my intention; he let it pass.

They let off steam for a while before I focused them on positives. I suggested that this was an ideal opportunity to approach our problems together. By pooling our thinking, we would create opportunities for making better use of all the available resources, whether people, machinery, space or anything else.

There was a lengthy silence, but it wasn't uncomfortable. I

hoped that the cynicism was disappearing. I asked Martin to update us on the office reallocation. The question surprised both Roland and Jim; as I suspected, the plan was news to them. Martin repeated what he had already told me, but this time he went further. I felt he had bottled this up for a long time.

'We need to have more discussion with staff to find out what they need. They are the ones doing the jobs yet there seem to be no channels for getting this over.'

It was then that Roland started to justify his presence: 'I need more computing support for the purchasing records. I'm sure we are wasting time re-keying stuff that's already in the computer and I bet that other departments are re-keying it again for their own use.'

Jim was mildly amused but already looking at his watch: 'Where do you want me to start? I've still got copies of all my reports. They didn't read them then . . .'

After a break for coffee I decided to risk a brainstorming session aimed at generating ideas for improvements. It worked superbly. Besides making suggestions about their own areas, they started crossing freely into other people's, and allowing others to cross into theirs. The list covered people's skills hidden or squashed; types of information needed to work more effectively; working relationships; offices; and equipment. Hardly any suggestions involved spending money, except in Jim's area which was going to be a hard nut to crack. One of the things to emerge for me was the complete breakdown in United's communication. No one knew what anyone else was doing. I thought that the meeting had been positive and I had gained a good start to my report. I suggested that we meet again in a week's time.

At that second meeting we started to piece together a really useful list of recommendations. I made sure that we included costings wherever possible, knowing that Mr Hines would pick holes in anything without them.

On the way home that evening I saw Arthur with Mr Hines in the car park. I don't know why exactly, but this seemed out of place.

Do you think that all this is practical? At times I think I'm going way beyond what Mr Hines wants from me. At others I can't help feeling that he must realize that serious change is long overdue.

My best regards

Andrew

Extract of letter from Michael to Andrew dated 31 March

. . . being creative is a two-way process that is often neglected. I've tried to come up with the opposite of creativity and I've found that it is complacency which is the provider of bad service and poor products. Complacency is the death of new ideas.

Your organization needs to plan its way forward, out of a period of decline, with deliberation and purpose. United Group has been too comfortable in the past. You will need to show skills of creativity and problem-solving in the weeks ahead.

You should be able to use pointers from my checklist in an opportunity which, I think, will come sooner rather than later.

- Be prepared to challenge existing methods and accepted wisdom. To some, such a challenge may appear excessive, to others you may not go far enough. I can only remind you of the sense of balance I've mentioned in the past.
- Make sure the objective of change is clear and worthwhile. Do not make changes for the sake of it.
- Create an atmosphere which is conducive to creativity and freedom of expression. Do not seek to dominate, impose or dictate your own ideas however convinced you are.
- Avoid possessiveness about ideas; encourage your team to share ideas and the ownership of them. For ideas to work they have to take hold and not be issued as mere instructions.
- Avoid negative reactions, even to impractical suggestions, by

listening carefully, by expressing appreciation, and by building on the ideas of others.

- There is a time and place for evaluation, criticism and selection of the good from the bad. This usually follows the creative process. Make sure your people understand the rules as well as you do.

- Remember that all successful products, services and improvements start as new ideas which have to take root. Think of the care needed for roots to grow.

THOU SHALT THINK CREATIVELY AND WELCOME NEW IDEAS

Michael

The Seventh Letters – Monitoring and Controlling

Relubbus

I am not pleased. The elephant's bum my have seemed a good idea, but all it did was provide a learning experience for Buckden; he has now established a base for real progress. I feel that your chances of destroying him are slipping away by the day. You have failed to identify the source of help he is receiving; it is beginning to have its effect. You have also signally failed to disturb the first six key activities in his process of management: there are only four more opportunities. I hope, for your sake, that you are able to grasp them.

Let us turn to the next phase in the assignment. It is not enough for managers to plan and issue instructions; after they have decided what must be done, they must check that it is happening, and take whatever steps are necessary to ensure that it does. This is the process of monitoring and control that should occupy a substantial proportion of the time of most practising managers.

It is not, of course, the role of managers to twiddle the knobs themselves, and this will (I am sure) suggest to you a first line of attack – to persuade the manager that he or she should do just that. There is little more destructive of morale than for the manager to seize the pen (or the keyboard, or whatever) from the hands of those

whose job it is to use it. To make this happen, you must persuade the manager that the task is not being well done, that he or she can do it better, and that the demands of the situation (time, accuracy, customer needs, demands from top management, legislative imperatives etc.) are so great that they must be met without fail. This should not take too much effort.

The consequences will be a delight to behold. The subordinates will be deeply resentful. They will feel they have been judged and found wanting. They will begrudge being denied the opportunity to show or develop the necessary skill. Best of all, it is probable that the manager will make a mess of the operation and end up needing the subordinate's help.

If managers have, despite our best efforts, planned effectively they will have set up an instrument by which they can monitor what is happening; a budget, for example, or a cash flow projection. Such aids make our task harder, but they will only cover the need to monitor – to find out and evaluate what is taking place. Control is another matter, and offers superb opportunities for mayhem.

All humans are guilt-ridden. This originates from their childhood experiences and relationships with their parents. It is reinforced throughout life by incidents which remind them of these – anything in which a higher authority sits in judgement over their behaviour. Any feeling that their actions are being monitored, let alone controlled, has guilt-raising potential for any human. Guilt thus lies at the root of management power.

In passing, it is worth noting that guilt is stimulated by threats of the supernatural. We have thus a direct part to play. Sadly, fewer managers are now worried by thoughts of what we have in store for them, but there are still opportunities. Grampound used to appear in dreams to his managers whenever they were feeling particularly doubtful about how they had done. Three of them were declared criminally insane, five were summarily dismissed for gross misconduct, and one resigned to take up basket weaving in Shetland. But Grampound had a genius for this, and I cannot recommend his approach for general application.

You have yourself been through the standard workshop on guilt-raising techniques, and if you were not fully proficient in them you would not have been chosen for your present assignment. This is an area in which The Curate has been especially useful in the past; you may wish to consider his use now.

Some managers, of course, need no guidance. They instinctively smell out the weaknesses, vulnerabilities and fears of their subordinates, and know exactly how to exploit them. They often gain a vice-like grip on their victims from which the latter cannot shake free – they become psychological slaves. Our involvement in such cases is confined to ensuring that the manager uses his or her power to harm and exploit the subordinate; fortunately, it is virtually certain that this will happen. In the best cases, managers with these skills become real dictators, capable of ruining the lives of fellow creatures with minimal help from us; they become 'Little Hitlers' (so named after one our most successful followers).

You may not yet have been indoctrinated into the most exciting work to come out of the ICM for many years – '55SM' (Fifty-Five Second Management). It is based on the management exploitation of guilt as a weapon of destruction, and has immense potential. As it is still under development, no manuals have yet been published, so I will now summarize the main action points for you. Commit the following pages to memory immediately on receipt, and then destroy by ingestion.

In its present form, there are three main branches of 55SM:

- 55-second blaming
- 55-second ridiculing
- 55-second confusing

55-second blaming

'Find someone doing something badly every day, and tell them so in no uncertain terms.' The concept of blame is itself an important one. You must ensure that when things go wrong (as they continually will) Buckden takes it for granted that someone must be to blame. If all else fails, you must ensure that he feels that he himself is to blame; this can, if necessary, always be combined with blaming others. For success in 55-seconds, the manager must:

1   Observe what is being done minutely. Ensure that the closeness of observation is noticed. Do this frequently and without explanation. Make the subordinate thoroughly nervous; if the task has been 'delegated' such scrutiny will be doubly disturbing.

2   Delay further action or explanation for as long as possible to convey the impression that serious action against the supposed offender is being planned. Small moves such as making a significant note, turning away pointedly, speaking to a third party in hushed tones, arranging a meeting without inviting the offender, or summoning a rival for discussion, can be effective.

3   Introduce the subject pompously and indirectly, implying that it has been given much thought, and that it is linked to a long chain of similar events. No clear statement about the cause for concern should be made, and general, threatening and indirect questions should be asked:
    'How do you feel about your current performance, Smith?' or 'Have you heard comments about your work recently, from colleagues?'

4   Launch into a tirade about whatever has been done, suggesting that it has wider implications than the offender could possibly understand, that it has been noted by senior people, and that its consequences cannot, at the present moment, be fully clarified.

5   Conclude the discussion by indicating that it will be necessary to think further about the incident, and that condign but ill-defined punishment will follow in due course.

6   Hold the episode against the offender indefinitely, referring to it

whenever his confidence shows signs of returning or he has done a particularly good job. Choose moments, as far as possible, when others are present.

55-second ridiculing

Ridicule works at two levels; by inspiring fear in the individuals ridiculed, and by uniting those who are not ridiculed on the side of the manager.

The procedure depends to a great extent on natural talent; some managers have a natural competence for ridiculing the efforts of their subordinates and colleagues. However, as in all other management activities, good training to agreed standards will be of benefit. The most effective procedure is:

1   Pick off the weakest. As every schoolchild knows, some individuals are natural targets for ridicule. The incompetent manager must be skilled at identifying and exploiting these. Unfortunately, we have lost some ground here. Aeons ago, it was sufficient to identify an individual as being of different religion, colour of skin or even sex, to make them appropriate targets. Whilst this remains possible, too many managers are now aware of the risks it entails.

Natural targets remain, nevertheless, easy to identify. All who suffer from unusual physical appearance, who are excessively tall, short or fat; all who appear clumsy or less bright; any who are known to hold minority opinions; any, of course, whose sexual preferences may be supposed to differ from the majority; the list is endless.

We are under attack here also; recent developments in what is known as 'politically correct' terminology suggest that 'fat' should be replaced by the non-discriminatory 'differently-sized', for example, and 'dead' by 'non-living'. However, the lads of ICM have great hopes that they will thwart its adoption, at least within the UK.

2   Limit the number of victims. Ridiculing can only form an effective means of managerial control if aimed at a small number of victims. Managers who attempt to ridicule too many of their subordinates will become the enemy of all.

3   Work indirectly. The manager should never confront the person to be ridiculed directly; ridiculing should be a matter of innuendo or carried out behind the victim's back. This strengthens the second benefit of the process – making others feel they are honoured by the confidence of the manager by being 'in on it'.

4   Use humour. Ridicule becomes boring if it sounds serious, and works best if the victim can be made an object of fun.

5   Beware of disloyalty. The manager should never sound disloyal to his people whilst ridiculing them. He must always make it clear that rumours he spreads have originated elsewhere; he is merely repeating the views of others in a non-malicious way, to show that he is aware of what goes on in his own area.

55-second confusing

You may doubt whether even the most ineffective manager could be persuaded that confusing subordinates was an efficient method of controlling them. It is true that confusing is not suitable for all situations. It is appropriate when managers believe they know best what to do and how to do it, and fear that subordinates may deliberately do something else. It is thus an excellent method for the dogmatic and self-opinionated when trying to control the independent and self-willed. The technique is as follows:

1.   Never set clear objectives. Confusion is made harder if objectives have been set.

2.   Never give instructions in writing. Some managers have mastered the art of writing confusing instructions, but this is a

rare skill. However, as Buckden's degree was in the humanities, the chances are still even that he possesses it.

3. Contradict yourself frequently. If nothing is in writing, it will be one person's word against another. After a while, subordinates will cease to trust their own memory and chronic confusion will ensue.

4. Keep your real intentions hidden. Success in confusion depends on steering those who might oppose the manager's wishes in as many conflicting directions as possible. Should they discover in which direction the manager is really aiming, they might use this to steer the other way.

5. Remain politically aware. If managers do not have objective standards, it will be easier for them to bend with the wind. Subordinates who do not understand the higher politics of the organization will find changes of direction incomprehensible. This approach was well exemplified by the vicar of the small parish of Bray near Windsor in England. That gentleman has now been in our care for several centuries.

    55SM can bring him within our reach.

Barripper

Garden Flat
Bristol
Thursday 27th April

Dear Michael

Thank you for your thoughts on my recent experiences. It's a relief to know that I'm on track after my earlier problems. Yet again, your latest letter is right on target. I begin to feel you really do have

second sight. How do you know which aspects of management are about to be most significant for me?

I remember what you said weeks ago about managing interruptions but before I tell you the latest episode in my saga, I must share something which is starting to worry me more than it should.

I have a dream which keeps coming back. I'm the master of an ocean liner sitting in state at my captain's table. Life is good. The orchestra is playing, and I am eating and drinking surrounded by important men and women, all of them looking up to me. Every so often, members of my crew come in with messages. A young officer tells me that he is concerned as there are reports of icebergs ahead. I tell him, in a voice everyone can hear, not to be so silly; there are never any icebergs at this time of year. Where, I ask him, did he learn his seamanship; in the Round Pond? Everyone at my table laughs, and the young officer goes away with his tail between his legs. After a while, the radio operator runs over to say that he has just received a message that there is a large berg five miles straight ahead. I smile at the ladies and ask which frequency it was received on, from which ship and whether the bearings allowed for both magnetic deviation and continental drift. Everyone laughs again, and the radio operator colours up and says he'll go back and check. Just as we get to the brandy and liqueurs, the first officer races in and shouts that the lookout has spotted a berg half a mile ahead. I jump up and tear him off a strip in front of everyone. I call him all the choicest sea-names I can think of, asking why he did not tell me earlier, why he did not alter course, and why he did not order the engines full astern. Just as I run out of things to throw at him, the ship smacks into something and water rushes in. As it lists over and starts to sink, I see everyone's eyes focused accusingly on me as they go under one by one. Just as the water reaches me, I wake . . . I've had the same dream five nights running now, and it's starting to get to me. . . .

I had one or two unpleasant problems with Joan over the last week or two, which haven't cheered me up. She doesn't seem good at layout, and I've made a habit of pointing out the mistakes she makes, in the hope that she will avoid them next time. Unfortunately, they don't seem to have got any less, and I rather lost my cool a week ago. I'd asked Joan to bring through a section of the draft report, and as soon as I saw it, I noticed that the margins were too narrow, and it was in single spacing, points I had mentioned to her only the day before.

'Haven't got the new word processor under control yet, have we?' I asked.

She didn't reply.

'Let's have a look at those margins,' I said.

She got up from her chair, and stood to one side, obviously indicating that I was welcome to sort them out. I'd forgotten which package she was using, and tried pressing 'shift' and 'f1', which was the set-up combination on my own pc. In fact, it came up with a message 'Define macro'. I hesitated, and went for the 'Escape' key. The result of this was a whirring, and the screen went blank.

'What does that mean?' I asked rather humbly.

'It means you've wiped off your draft and the rest of my afternoon's work.'

I apologized as abjectly as I could, and brought in a large bunch of flowers next morning. The episode may not have improved her layout, but I think it's taught me something about managing people.

Arthur came to see me later that day. He accused me of holding meetings behind his back and told me to keep off his patch. I told him that I had invited him to the meetings and pointed out that he had received copies of all our paperwork. He replied that Martin was too inexperienced; he still needed firm control. I had no intention of upsetting him. I said that our discussions were not important enough to require his personal involvement. He ignored that and asked what exactly was going on. He was trying to make out that there was a conspiracy against him. Trying to be positive, I asked whether he had had the opportunity to read our draft reports, and what he thought of the progress we had made. All he could was to criticize Martin. He said that he had to reprimand Martin only the other day for discussing office moves with Sue, instead of using the proper channels. That, of course, meant him. I asked if Martin's discussions with Sue had been useful, but Arthur was not to be put off. He told me that was not the point and that he would have to keep a much tighter rein on Martin in the future. This was beginning to get me; proper delegation and use of individual strengths were to be a key feature of the report. I saw no point in continuing. Nor indeed did Arthur as he turned on his heel and left without further comment. I felt for Martin. I had made his life difficult by involving him.

I was beginning to compose my thoughts when Mr Hines barged in and asked me 'how things were progressing'. I nearly asked him what 'things' he meant, but decided it was wiser to be vague.

'Everything's fine,' I said blandly.

His next shot took the wind out of my sails.

'I understand you've been pestering Arthur for a change of office. You should leave decisions of that kind to him.'

I couldn't believe what I was hearing and fell back on explanation.

'It's just that I need to be closer to Marketing and Accounts. It takes me nearly ten minutes to walk across to see Alan or Sue.'

'Two small points Andrew. One – please remember there is such a device as a telephone. Two, and more importantly, I have to tell you that one or two of your colleagues have mentioned that you are already seeing a good deal of Ms Archer, despite the ten-minute walk.'

To say that I was flabbergasted would be the understatement of the century. As he moved towards the door I tried desperately to regain solid ground.

'Can I tell you about progress on the report? I'm including a section on pollution and environmental management that I'm working on with Jim.'

'What report's that? Uh, yes, yes. Not now. Get my secretary to diary something in.'

With that he left.

The two visits left me in a sombre mood. They had only lasted five minutes but they had both left me feeling guilty. It was ironic because I was just writing up some of Martin's comments and I still felt bad that I'd put him in an even more difficult position with Arthur. So many good ideas had come from Martin. He had blossomed in our meetings. On one occasion he had stunned Jim to silence with his ideas on the value of people's contributions. I looked down at my notes: 'How do you measure the value of someone who is fun to work with, and helps others to do their jobs better?' he had asked. 'How do you measure the contribution of a new idea, or suggestion? A £10 cheque for an idea adopted from the suggestion box is almost an insult. At the moment good ideas are squashed if they don't stick to the right "procedure".'

It was Martin who had pointed out that management need to share responsibility with authority and trust. He had become quite outspoken about Arthur peering over his shoulder all the time. I looked at my notes again: 'If we are to become more responsible for what we are doing, we must have an atmosphere in which people can discuss and criticize without fear of being punished.' As you say in your letter, it's all a question of balance. I wondered if Jim or Roland had ever been on the receiving end of an Arthur outburst, or a Hines' intrusion.

I've come to rely a good deal on Sue. Her help has been invaluable. It was Sue who suggested that my working party needed to follow up the resource inventory with some guidelines on managing people which Martin contributed so ably. I had no idea that Hines, or anyone else for that matter, had been keeping tabs on us. She's a lovely girl, but even I am not stupid enough to get involved.

Later, when I was drafting a section on managing people, Hines' secretary rang to say that my report was now wanted by 12 June. Yet another unexplained change, but I could still just about make it. I asked for a quick meeting to discuss progress but she said that Mr Hines was completely tied up for the next ten days . . . I suppose I expected something like this.

Although my report is beginning to take on real substance, my boss's interventions make me wonder if I am signing my own death-warrant. But I'm still optimistic because the report will be at least supported by four signatures, not just one.

I look forward to your next letter.

My best wishes

Andrew

Extract of letter from Michael to Andrew dated 20 April

. . . so monitoring and control should be more about helping your people to meet their targets than checking output statistics or counting productivity measures. Of course you must check that things are getting done; the trick is to avoid treating subordinates as inferior. I realize that problems of this kind may come from your boss as well as from subordinates. I know this can cause endless headaches, but think of the standards you set for yourself and persevere with your boss in discussion. Think of the dripping tap; keep him informed; question his view with respect and follow the path he has set you with honesty and consistency. The aim is not to find a colleague to ridicule or a victim to blame, but rather a cooperative atmosphere where goals can be shared and achieved. As before I'll close with a summary:

- Ensure that appropriate standards and targets are understood, but be sensitive to changes from those standards. Don't become over-sensitive – there could be a number of reasons.
- Beware that monitoring does not become damaging to motivation. Acknowledge when targets are met and be appreciative when work is well done. Monitoring is not a case of peering over shoulders, or spying; it is open, agreed and shared.
- Ask yourself, and your boss, the following questions. The answers are often surprising:

    - Are you approachable when there is a problem?

- Are you ready and willing to listen?
- Are you good at motivating others?
- Are you consistent, honest and fair?
- Are you able to maintain discipline?
- Are you prepared to make decisions?
- Are you respectful and able to praise when praise is due?
- Are you good at keeping your word?

- Last but not least – do not create the impression that failure implies blame. Focus on the positive aspects and be supportive to get performance back on track.

THOU SHALT MONITOR AND CONTROL THE PROGRESS OF THINE OPERATION AGAINST THY PLAN

Michael

The Eighth Letters – Leadership

Dear Relubbus

Your attempt to use dream control techniques with Buckden was certainly interesting, but I suspect that its success will be limited. As I warned you, such methods are not for use by inexperienced operators. However, full marks for a brave try.

Once again, your success has been limited. Buckden has overcome the obstacles you set in monitoring the work of his secretary. I am now certain that Buckden is receiving help from a source you have so far failed to trace. This is now your top priority; continued failure to identify this would prove catastrophic, not for Buckden, but for you.

The number of opportunities open to you is becoming frighteningly small; one of the few left is in the area of leadership. Management and leadership have much in common, but they are not the same. You must now consider leadership in its own right. Buckden is currently in charge of only a secretary. There is, however, the possibility that he may, at any moment, be given a real leadership role. Like most newly-appointed managers, he has received no guidance or training to equip him for this. Like many, he was made a manager because of his qualifications, without any thought for leadership qualities.

On the morning of his appointment, his boss said 'Well done', introduced him to his secretary, gave him the keys to a company car, and left him alone in his new office. If all goes as it should, you can ensure that his organization has lost an effective manager and gained a poor leader.

How can you best go about this? An ancient Chinese busybody (whose sayings deserve oblivion) once stated that people's reaction to leaders could be distinguished on the following scale. They

- Hate   the worst
- Fear   the next worst
- Dispute with   the next
- Honour   the next best
- Don't notice   the best

Clearly your job is to ensure that Buckden is seen at the top of this list. Here are some hints on how to make this happen.

You will know that when we want humans to commit atrocities, we persuade them that their victims are not real people, but members of a class of sub-humans. We suggest that they do not live in the same kind of house, or eat the same food. We hint that they may have peculiar habits such as wearing bedsocks or smelling their own armpits. We tell them that such beings do not think and feel as they do. We ensure that the torturers never realize that their victims have families, homes, hopes and fears just like theirs. 'Moral principles' (as humans call them) cannot, we point out, apply in dealings with such beings.

This thinking is central to our teaching about leadership. People hate and fear those who make them feel non-human. As always, we start with words. Emphasize, for example, the significance of the term 'subordinates'. They used to be called 'hands'; the word 'inferiors', is quite nice, but lacks some of the flavour of the older word. Whilst 'other ranks', 'junior staff', and 'the lads' now do a similar job, they too lack bite.

Humans attach unbelievable importance to their own name. Its sound is music to their ears. Ideally, therefore, managers should be taught never to use their subordinates' names. The armed forces are our best pupils, compelling lower ranks to use numbers and address each other as 'Soldier', 'Bombardier' or 'Sir' as the case may be. We have temporarily lost ground in civilian circles, but there are still one or two ploys available to us.

Managers with poor memories will forget their people's names; Buckden may be one of these. Arrange for him to pass his subordinates in the corridor or the workshop without recognizing or acknowledging them. Persuade him that if he looks important, in a hurry, or generally too busy this will enhance their respect.

As an amusing variation, you may get Buckden to mix people up. Our most inventive tempters can ensure that their managers confuse both the names and jobs of their subordinates. In 1986, Bradnop permanently discombobulated his manager over the names and responsibilities of all eight of his subordinates. He was able to maintain the situation indefinitely by persuading him it was accepted as a manifestation of his acknowledged pre-eminence.

Managers with a public school background (or even more those who wish to make out they have one) can be persuaded to use surname only – 'Smith, come to my office, will you'.

Hate will be strongest for managers who indicate that their people's contribution is neither known or valued. You must ensure that Buckden expresses no interest in or appreciation of anything his people have done. Small actions will do the trick nicely. Faint and obviously insincere praise, a disparaging tone of voice, negative facial expressions and body language all help. Shuffling papers about on his desk, glancing at his watch or his diary; anything to show he is not listening. Impatience is a great asset – let him never quite have the time to listen, especially to descriptions of his people's successes. If he is forced to listen, ensure that he quickly forgets, or better still later ascribes success to the wrong person. The most powerful effect will be produced when he claims the success for himself.

Two powerful weapons in producing hate are self-importance and shyness. By developing Buckden's self-importance it should be possible, whenever a crisis arises, such as a child's illness or a parent's death, to convince him that he has more important matters to attend to. Compassionate leave should be granted grudgingly, with an indication that it implies weakness and is almost certainly no more than swinging the lead.

Shyness is frequently mistaken for snobbishness, and the image of a shy manager can easily be distorted into that of one who is stuck up and stand-offish. Bad leaders give nothing of themselves to their subordinates. But people like to feel they know those with power over them, and will feel the need to invent what they are not told. You should be aware of our character-assassination pack, which can be mixed and matched according to need. It includes rumours that the manager:

- is having it off with his/her secretary
- has a son in Pentonville
- is on hard drugs

and many other amusing notions. With sufficient ingenuity, you are certain to find some groundless scandal that can be made to stick on Buckden. Only last year, our efforts persuaded colleagues of a hard-working but shy manager of impeccable integrity, a pillar of his Baptist Chapel and a local magistrate, that he was under investigation for repeated indecent exposure on the London Underground.

Any symptoms of effective decision-making must be taken seriously. This is a dangerous condition, which can lead rapidly to a raising of the sufferer's credibility as a leader. The disease invades the central nervous system, and causes a progressive paralysis of the entire process of destruction, which, if not treated early, proves fatal to our plans. Fortunately the disease is rare in managers. The only effective treatment is based on a controversial technique known as Concentrated Self-Delusory Hypnosis (CSDH). Whilst the concept is fairly straightforward its use requires proper training and is not for the enthusiastic amateur. For this reason, it can only be practised by those with the CSDH diploma. You should go on one of the five-day practitioner seminars as soon as possible, although I should warn you that they are expensive, and my training budget is now exhausted.

Concentrated Self-Delusory Hypnosis begins by studying the eye movements of the manager during decision making. The direction in which he or she most frequently looks indicates his or her predominant mode of thought. The indications are:

- Up right   hasty
- Up left   helpless
- Level right   apathetic
- Straight ahead   prevaricating
- Level left   confused
- Down right   painstaking
- Down left   scientific
- Both shut   fast asleep

CSDH next sets about creating a delusion that exaggerates the manager's natural tendencies. Thus a hasty decision-maker will be programmed to believe that a macho leader makes decisions such as 'Where should we build our new production facility?' instantaneously. Painstaking decision-makers must be persuaded that people will only follow them if they examine every possibility exhaustively and at enormous length, preferably using sheets of flip chart paper, markers and masking tape. Prevaricating decision-makers will be guided to hold endless unstructured team meetings without agenda or objectives. Scientific decision-makers will be shown that even simple yes/no decisions, such as 'Should we let the staff off an hour early on Christmas Eve?' require the most rarefied and complex procedures, using incomprehensible mathematical modelling and the most sophisticated technology.

Another sure way to ensure managers are feared and hated is to get them to cheat. The phrases 'cheating on your wife', 'cheating on your partner' are now generally accepted. From a study of over a thousand managers, MDU has constructed a leadership model based on the concept of leaders 'cheating on their subordinates'. Their report constitutes a goldmine of cheating behaviour observable in a large proportion of managers. Amongst the commonest are:

- Taking credit due to subordinates
- Blaming subordinates for their own mistakes

- Withholding necessary information from subordinates
- Failing to support subordinates under external attack
- Criticizing subordinates publicly
- Denying subordinates merited promotion
- Overworking willing subordinates
- Not consulting subordinates about changes which will affect them

Copies of a checklist are available from the MDU. Try each out on Buckden at a suitable opportunity, stressing the immediate advantages each offers. The drawbacks are less obvious, and there is every probability that he will have moved on (downwards or, if you have otherwise failed, upwards) before they are noticed.

Finally, a word about some of the excellent leadership training that is now provided by the ICM. The two most popular workshops are: the Passive-Centred Leader (PCL) and the Homeward Bound Courses (HBC).

The Passive-Centred Leader depends on the magical properties of three intersecting circles. The first represents the ego of the manager, the second the difficulties facing him or her, and the third the incompetence of his or her team. Only when the three fully overlap will total chaos result; the training provides instruments for assessing the present situation and how best to achieve the desired result. The workshop ends with a syndicate exercise using old bedsocks to build a model of the Taj Mahal. Participants take away a small plastic card depicting the intersecting circles. This has two uses; if gazed at intently it produces a hypnotic trance in which participants believe themselves once again to be members of their syndicate at the workshop; and it can also be used for opening Yale-type locks.

Homeward Bound Courses bring a group of managers from diverse backgrounds together in a large tank submerged just off Prawle Point in the Bristol Channel. The group is split into three and a half, and given a number of tasks to complete. Typically these will include: finding out why on earth each member is there, seeing whether individuals are able to climb round the inside of the tank

without touching the floor (none have yet done so), trying to attract the attention of the nearest lifeboat station, and sitting motionless for as long as possible. The benefits, in terms of improved management effectiveness, are widely attested.

This is a fascinating field. Your time, and my patience, are both running low.

Barripper

Garden Flat
Bristol
Tuesday 19 May.

Dear Michael

Thank you for your last letter. It was a godsend. Your comments on recent events are invaluable. I shall get hold of the article on management style you recommended. You tell me to put doubt and confusion behind me and push on ahead with my report. Recently I had to use some of the techniques you listed in your recent letters. I needed all the leadership skills I could muster in this latest episode.

I had been planning to spend some time in Production with Jim. There was still a large gap in my report on his area, especially the aspect of possible environmental damage. I had arranged to see Jim to try and get some facts from him, but once again, events took an unexpected turn.

A week ago I had a phone call from Sue to ask me to take over the Open Day because she had been sent on a training course by Mr Hines. I was pleased to be asked, but a little wary too. The deadline for my report was looming and although I had some horrible premonitions about its outcome, I knew it would be even worse if I didn't finish it on time. I wondered what I was letting myself in for.

Sue's plans certainly appeared thorough although I did not know all the names assigned for roles. This was her team, and I wondered how well they would work for me. I was relieved to see Alan's name, daunted to see Peter Plews' and sceptical about Jim. There were questions marks against Arthur and Martin. After recent events with Arthur I had my own doubts about Martin's participation.

Sue's flair for organization had produced a promising mix of formality and informality which should make for an interesting day. The question was – could I now put it together? There were several names I didn't know. It was vital that they accept me as team-leader and not a second choice. Equally important was my ability to motivate them. Going over Sue's plans again the date struck me – there was only one week to go.

Martin was due to act as a guide through the central complex. I wasn't sure whether Arthur was off that day or if Sue had decided not to ask him. Martin was a little wary when he saw me. He was keen to take part but he didn't know if it was going to cause more bad blood with Arthur. I made a mental note to see Arthur and marked Martin down as a 'not sure'.

Lady Grazier was assigned the opening welcome. This was a risk. She was respected throughout the organization but it was well-known that she took on a lot of public engagements. She would be willing of course but it was more a question of making sure she got there on time.

Roland Brown in Purchasing wasn't on Sue's list but he had made it to two of my resource meetings and had proved helpful. As it turned out, he didn't 'have the time at such short notice', especially as the resources project was giving him 'far more to do'. There was nothing I could say. At the end of the day I had a plan, a headache and the makings of a team. Would they accept me as team-leader?

That night I had a nightmare. Everything had gone wrong. It had been a shambles. I saw distributors tearing up contracts and customers leaving early shaking their heads; I saw groups lost in the corridor as Arthur withdrew Martin at the last minute; I saw the MD arrive as the last group left for the factory visit; I saw Ronald Kettlewell joking loudly about my unhelpfulness and how he'd put me right; I saw the face of a devil leering at me. I thought I'd seen that face before but I couldn't place it. I felt he had planned this disaster. The mess, however, was mine alone. It was my responsibility. I had let United down because I hadn't been able to carry out Sue's plan and galvanize the staff into a good performance. The devil's face mouthed 'Bungler' silently at me as Mr Hines watched from behind. I woke up in a cold sweat.

That was when I decided to get on with making a good job of it. That morning I looked at the plan again; it would work. But if I needed cooperation I had to start by showing that I was in charge and that we were going to do a good job of presenting the company.

Ignoring all interruptions, I spent the next morning drafting presentations and notes and making phone calls. I passed my drafts through to Joan and asked her to turn them into something presentable.

I called on Martin and asked if he'd given it further thought.

He still didn't know: 'It's Arthur. I think he'd handcuff me to the desk if he could. Yesterday he gave me enough paperwork to shuffle until the year 2000.'

I realized how difficult I had made things for him. I had to see Arthur urgently.

Arthur was on the telephone when I called. Someone was giving him a rough time. He was overdue with some report or other, I wondered if it was about office reallocation.

'Arthur, I would value your opinion on that draft report that I've been putting together for Mr Hines. It needs someone fresh to look at it. We've been getting too close to it. I thought you were the best person to give us an informed comment.'

He was still reeling from his phone call.

'OK. I'll get to it when I can. I can't promise anything in the next week. I'm up to my eyes.'

I thanked him and made to leave.

'Oh, by the way,' I hesitated by the door, 'there's something I'd really appreciate your help with.' I was taking a risk, but a calculated risk.

I waited as Arthur made the effort to look up again.

'Sue's asked me to do the Open Day and I'm dreadfully short of experienced people. Could you see your way to . . .'

He cut in: 'Not a chance. Sue spoke to me about it. There's no way I can find the time.' He fell right into the trap.

'But we do need someone from your area who has inside knowledge of the central complex, and can explain its workings to the visitors. After all, it's the key to everything else . . .'

I paused for a few moments, to let the flattery sink in, hoping he might suggest the solution I wanted.

'If you really can't make it . . .' I paused again; there was silence.

'Is there any chance you could release Martin for a couple of hours?'

He grunted: 'Provided that it is no more than that. When is it?'

'Next Monday.'

The conversation was over. I thanked him and promised to keep him in the picture. As I left I wondered if my victory was going to cause Martin still more problems. Somehow I didn't think so. Arthur looked really harassed.

Joan had fixed a meeting for all those taking part. I knew I wouldn't get a second chance as I addressed twenty-five faces in the Conference Room. The atmosphere was cold.

'Thank you all for coming at such short notice and thank you for offering to be key players in making a success of the Open Day. I know I am a newcomer to this like some of you but I think we have a marvellous opportunity and I know we can pull it off. First let me tell you what I propose.

I shall be at the Welcome. If the MD can't make it at the last minute I shall give her introduction. After that, I shall be on walkabout all day – not to interfere – but as a support, and to muck in as needed . . . I thought I might introduce all the presentations and set the scene for them – I feel a brief introduction is always helpful to the speaker. To save you work, I've prepared drafts for the presentations. Please go over them and feel completely free to make any changes you want, or use your own material if you prefer. I know Martin has his. I'm having the 35mm projector serviced this week, but I shall have another in reserve.'

I saw them thawing a little.

'Joan, at the end of the welcome would you make sure that our guests know where they can find a telephone or fax to contact home or work. They'll all have a programme and brief plan of the complex and the guides will all have bleepers to call me in case of need. After that would you spend the day in the Conference Room to assist the presentations?

'Martin, I've looked over your outline. It's good. I've made one or two comments but you handle it the way you propose.

'Alan, I'd like you to take the first presentation, followed by Peter. I will do a brief summary before lunch, and then the guides can see everyone gets to the Dining Room.

'Peter, thanks for taking the hard one on marketing in Sue's absence. I understand you are OK for material?'

Peter nodded and asked how we should deal with questions we couldn't answer, or any complaints. I could see they were waiting to see what I would say.

'If you don't know the answer to a question, there's no harm in saying so. Don't flannel or get embarrassed; tell them that you'll find out and make sure you get back to them before they leave. I hope our guests won't have any complaints, but if they do, please let me know at once, and I'll take over from there.' I remembered Mr Kettlewell and his gnomes. 'Whatever you do, don't say that it's another department, or somebody else's fault. It is important to show that we are all working together.'

They looked relaxed. I was winning.

'OK, please take a couple of minutes to see if there's anything I've missed.'

Amidst the hubbub Martin asked me what Arthur had said about him taking part. I confirmed that he had agreed, and a smile spread over his face.

'I won't ask how you did it,' he said.

Before closing I called a further meeting in two days when we would go over our roles and try a dummy run of the presentations. I looked round; some were talking, some were making notes. It was going to work.

During the rest of the week, I rehearsed with Joan, and Martin when he could get away. I checked routes, timings and equipment until I felt sure that I had control of the plan.

The Open Day was a success. The MD arrived on time for her welcome and everything worked from first to last. I had last-minute worries about Peter Plews swapping his marketing hat for his more familiar industrial relations one but Joan told me that his presentation went down very well. Jim found time to do an excellent job of shielding the guests from the worst of our Production horrors. When the last visitor had gone I thanked everyone individually for their contribution. Back in the office I had a special word of thanks to Joan who had worked like a Trojan all day.

Two days later I received this note from Lady Grazier:

Congratulations to all those who played an active part in making the Open Day the success it was. Sales enquiries have already risen. Well done to you all.

I asked Joan to circulate it to everyone who had helped.

I recalled what you said about leadership. Am I getting there?

Thank you once again

Andrew

Extract of letter from Michael to Andrew dated 11 May

. . . of ink has been spilt on the question of whether leaders are born or made. I trust you now appreciate that there are certain characteristics, common to great leaders of the past, other than charisma or inspiration, which are vital to successful leadership in today's unstable working environment. Do not be fooled by the simplicity of the questions in my last letter – it's harder that you think!

I sense that you are about to embark on a project which will test your leadership skills in a situation that will be new to you. There will be new faces, new names and new demands. You don't have to be a master of everything your people do; work more on providing the right conditions for them to be productive.

- Learn the names of your people and get to know them. They should recognize that you are willing to get stuck in and take your share of the action.
- Learn when to help and when not to; when to listen, when to suggest and when to compromise; learn when to step back and manoeuvre, and when to instruct and confront.
- Recognize and use the skills and abilities of all members of the team. Try to support, encourage and develop them without being patronizing.
- Avoid phrases such as 'It's not my department' and see problems as opportunities for everyone to shine. Problems don't usually go away so you may as well tackle them with gusto.
- Remember that you have to manage upwards, sideways and down; it's not just subordinates, but colleagues and boss as well.
- Harry Truman said: 'The buck stops here.' In my last letter I said that you must be prepared to make decisions. You must take responsibility for them too. You will make bad decisions as well as good ones. The important thing is to know why you've taken them and where they will lead you.
- Do not try to appear omniscient; you are not. Do not forget the values of honesty and integrity; they will stand you in greater stead than feigned cleverness.
- Understand the process of making things happen through others. Some call it facilitating, others enabling or empowering. I prefer to call it helping.

THOU SHALT LEAD THY PEOPLE WELL AND HELP
THEM DEVELOP TOWARD THEIR FULL STATURE

Michael

The Ninth Letters – The Environment

Relubbus

As you know, it has been my desperate desire and constant aim in these letters to guide and help you in your efforts to ruin the management career of Andrew Buckden. I have to say that my pessimism about the success of your efforts is rapidly turning to desperation. I can do nothing about the reports that the Watchers will have made to Infernal Security (IS).

That you tried, despite my twice-repeated advice, to use the Dream Technique, and that alone, I find totally inexplicable. That you failed abysmally, and allowed Buckden to lead the Open Day as he did, was inevitable. You have paid the penalty for trying to fly before you are able to crawl.

Time is now running out, but my experience tells me that all is not yet finally lost. We have still to exploit the most fruitful field of all; one in which our powers have been exalted to the point of triumph, and by working in which we will destroy not merely our managers' insignificant careers, but through them the entire human race and their precious earth itself. I refer, of course, to the effects of what these pompous, petty little people do to the environment in which they and their subordinates, families, customers and indeed the whole boiling of them must live.

This is our master plan. It is through this that we will doom their entire race to a slow, painful and degrading extinction. It is in the achievement of this destruction that the All Lowest will show His power and those of us privileged to have served Him will see the final flowering of our efforts. And it is through this that those of us who have striven so long and, I may say, so cunningly, in the Management Destruction Unit will demonstrate that our work has not been marginal or subordinate, but at the very heart of the All Lowest's planning.

But to specifics. Your crash course in terrestrial history will have shown you how we have used managers, from the start of the 'industrial revolution' as the prime agents of the progressive degradation and destruction of their own environment. You will have been taught the various elements in this process. How, at the very beginning, we arranged for the use of renewable sources of energy – wind, water and dead vegetation – to be supplanted by irreplaceable fossil fuels and also hid the consequences of this for about two hundred years. How we ensured that for over a century the nature of the waste generated, whether during manufacturing or after use of the product, was regarded as unworthy of attention. How we persuaded managers that packaging and the throw-away mentality were essential for generating sales, whatever resources it consumed, whatever size the mountains of non-degradable plastic produced and whatever the immensity of the forests of irreplaceable timber that were destroyed. The glorious list is long.

Much remains to be done. Too many fields are still unpolluted, too many rivers still support fish, too many wild flowers still grow. Inspire Buckden with some new, wasteful or polluting idea and your chances of demotion will be changed at a stroke.

You will have heard of the 'green movement', and how it has gathered strength through the last decade. You will be aware of the numerous forays of this ideology into management. You may have been misled into thinking that our Plan has at length been rumbled, and like so many humans, you may believe that the whistle has been blown on our game. If so, how profoundly you and they will share an error! It is not for nothing that Grindalythe was the first member of the MDU to be lowered to the dignity of Archtempter. It is through the combination of his genius and unremitting efforts against implacable and uncomprehending opposition that the green movement was conceived, brought into existence and raised to its present status. Let me explain.

To outsiders, the green movement appears to endanger the triumph of our strategy for the destruction of the human environment. In fact, it is the opposite. It is a main shield, protection and support to our Plan, and will ensure its rapid progress to the conclusion we so earnestly desire. The profound cleverness of this approach, which has only gradually been appreciated outside the MDU, lies in the fact that managers (and others) should be deeply concerned about the protection of the environment. But what we have hidden is that the nature of that concern, and of the actions it generates, are what matters.

The more powerful the emotion, the greater the damage it can cause. Individuals who are emotionally involved see only extremes, and see others only as with them or against them. We have used this principle throughout human history. We have twisted well-founded concern for the misuse of wealth and power into political beliefs which have killed millions and set the large areas of the world back by a hundred years. We have perverted a legitimate belief in liberty into lawlessness and anarchy. We have transmuted concern for morality into cruel tyranny. Compared with these achievements, using care for the environment to destroy what it seeks to protect is simple.

The green movement will achieve this by:

- distracting attention from our main thrust
- confusing thinking about the real issues
- making rational management decision-making harder
- generating destructive conflict between nations and areas of the world
- producing misleading measures of progress
- deepening mistrust between productive industry and the rest of the community
- stimulating fanaticism

and in other ways too numerous to mention here.

In fact, the very concept of 'green concerns' is a misnomer. Grindalythe has cunningly ensured that issue after issue has been added to the list, in such a way that it is now all but impossible to identify which are central, which are subordinate and which are completely out of place. The original issues involved pollution of rivers, then soil, the atmosphere and the ocean. Pollution from atomic weapons and power were an obvious and highly emotive special case. To these he added worries about the exhaustion of finite resources, especially fossil fuels. Destruction of the ozone layer came next, together with the effects of the build-up of 'greenhouse gases' (a delightfully descriptive phrase due to his assistant Catrigge). Grindalythe's attempt to add pollution by noise to the list has so far been only partly successful. The use of chemical fertilizers is an issue with unexploited potential, but chemical pesticides and weed-killers have done well for us. Wine lakes and butter mountains are perpetual winners.

But the greatest potential at the present time lies in issues connected with man's fellow creatures. The loss of what they call 'wildlife' and the sufferings of farm animals are of increasing interest and promise well. Grindalythe has plans to move as rapidly as possible into the area of insects.

As you will understand, each of these concerns is in fact of the gravest importance to humans; Grindalythe's strategy depends upon confusing them and their followers together in such a way that labels are confused, priorities are mixed, and loyalties are at loggerheads. Recent international attempts to mobilize political support for green concerns illustrate this perfectly.

You may be asking what this has to do with Buckden's success as a manager. My reply is 'everything'. Buckden is currently unconcerned about environmental matters, except insofar as they may be embodied in legislation. You must raise his awareness, and with it his emotional involvement. Get him to start asking questions:

- 'If we gave all staff mobile phones and laptop computers, would the reduction of heating and lighting costs produce a net saving in energy costs?'
- 'Should all company cars be converted to run off the methane produced by the local pig farm?'
- 'Should all computer and clerical staff be put on night shift, to benefit from half-price electricity?'
- 'Should the figures of water consumption per head in the toilets be monitored department by department, and a league table be published regularly?'
- 'Should we refuse to accept electricity, some of which may have been generated by nuclear power?'
- 'Should all personnel be given three months to become vegetarian or face dismissal?'
- 'Would the generation of our own electricity by means of windmills erected on the directors' car park be more environmentally friendly than a water wheel supplied by the overflow from the works urinal?'

I am sure that more similar questions will occur to you. Whilst not all will be useful in practice, the aggravation caused by searching for answers will be worth the effort. Buckden's credibility will also be steadily but surely eroded. Even more importantly, such petty and unimportant questions will be seen as typifying green concerns, and major issues will remain unconsidered.

If, despite this, larger questions of the environment are raised, either by Buckden or his colleagues, you must fall back on our second strategy: ensure that, in correcting one problem, another of greater seriousness is created. In environmental matters, this is so easy that it will often happen even without our intervention. Thus, whilst ensuring that no substances that have been tested on animals are used, it is probable that one alternative will use four times as much energy and another break down after use into highly toxic waste matter.

Our third strategy is to build a link between concern for the environment and politics. Grindalythe has succeeded here too. You should be aware that several developed countries already have a Green Party which has sought election at local and national level. Whilst it probably aims to stand apart from the established right-left political spectrum, Grindalythe has ensured its identification in the minds of most voters with the left. This has naturally tainted the issues and policies it seeks to promote in the eyes of those of other persuasions, and made them less likely to be embraced by society as a whole.

Buckden's political opinions do not appear to have been recorded in his personal file. Find out what they are so that you know how to approach him on this issue. If he tends towards the right, point out the irresponsible, disorganized, trendy nature of the green movement. If he tends towards the left, enlist him as a paid-up member, and ensure he mentions the fact in the senior dining room. We win either way.

My time, my patience and your opportunities are all but exhausted.

Barripper

Garden Flat
Wednesday 3 June.

Dear Michael

Thank you for your comments on the Open Day. For me it was a time when much of what we have discussed came together. I enjoyed it enormously and got a real sense of achievement from it. It has delayed the completion of my report but I'm still within the deadline that Mr Hines has set. After the hustle and bustle of the Open Day, I had to force myself to focus on the report again. By the time you get this letter it will be virtually complete, so my fate will be sealed.

As your unbelievable second sight has already told you, the environment has jumped to the top of my agenda. Your letter on environmental matters arrived after it all started, but it was good to know that I was already on the right track. Let me tell you how it happened.

Richard, Laura's nephew, is just twelve, and comes to stay with us often enough to regard the spare bedroom as his own. For the last few months, it was nothing but sports cars. About three weeks ago, this all changed. Tentative enquiries started about advance Christmas presents, and it took only a little probing to establish that fishing kit was now the key to Heaven. Memories of idyllic hours by the Bootle canal twenty years ago flooded back, as the two of us took our place together on the river bank that Saturday afternoon.

'What's that, Uncle Andrew?' Richard asked, after about fifteen minutes of inactivity.

'Looks like a dead fish, to me,' I replied.

'Another dead fish,' he commented, five minutes later.

'No wonder I'm not getting any bites,' he said after another short while.

'Looks like they're all dead in this river.'

In the first hour, we counted twenty-three very dead fish floating by, belly up. We decided to call it a day.

I called in on Jim first thing on Monday. He still hadn't got round to costing the replacement equipment which Mr Hines had asked him about months ago, but he told me that Roland in Purchasing had secured some good tenders. A quick glance at the figures convinced me that the capital expenditure would be far less than Jim had been spending on maintenance and repair. I at last managed to steer the conversation round to the environment, and the possible damage that Jim's crumbling operation was causing. The subject was a complete unknown to me. Of course I have read the fiction about how we take a year off the life of the planet every time we have a bath, but apart from a newspaper article mentioning new regulations from the Environmental Protection Agency I did not know where to start.

Some years ago, Jim told me, there had been a hushed–up dispute with the local Environmental Health Department. A lot of fish in the river had died, and it was suspected that discharges from our plant had been the cause. Nothing had been proven, but there has been some bad publicity and Jim had written a report for the Board indicating that waste levels discharged in the river were unacceptably high. Jim complained that writing a report was the end of anything worthwhile. I thought that ominous. However, he seemed genuinely to welcome my involvement.

There were a number of things I had to do. Firstly I had to find just how much we were damaging the environment. Jim's old study was a starting point, although the information would have to be updated. Secondly, we needed some hard information on what the regulations and controls now were, and what changes were coming out and when. Controls would be much tighter today than they had been three or four years ago and I wondered if they would be enforceable by law. If so, what were the penalties for non-compliance? How much time did we have?

I asked Jim if he would monitor current discharge levels as a top priority. He wasn't too keen on a full series of tests, but he accepted that they had to be done, and promised results by the end of the week. The second task – the research – was all mine. And I still wasn't sure where to begin.

I thought of the local Environmental Health Office as the obvious place to start, but Jim and I agreed that it wouldn't be too clever to alert them to our fears at this stage.

When I got back to my office, a memo was lying on my desk:

To: A. Buckden Esquire

Re: THE ENVIRONMENT

I understand you are taking a good look at United Group's Environmental Standards. I hope you will not take it amiss if I offer my humble suggestions as to how the United Group Directors and Senior Managers should be tackling the Problem. I do not require any Acknowledgement or Recognition for this, which should in any case be given to my Superiors such as you.

I have the following Valuable Ideas to suggest, Viz:

- *you should check how much water everyone uses in the Staff toilets*
- *a night-shift for office-workers from which there would be enormous benefits from Cut-Price electricity*
- *windmills, which were good enough for our Ancestors and should be good enough for us*
- *only Animal-Free food in the Canteen*

I remain, Sir, your obedient Humble servant.

A. Well-Wisher

Who on earth had sent this? I asked Joan if she had any idea where it had come from. She made a sign indicating that he was a screwball and carried on with her work. The night–shift suggestion at least made me think of the practicalities of homeworking. This was the only suggestion I received.

Joan had mentioned United's Information Centre, commenting that she had never been there. I was annoyed that this was yet another area that had been excluded from my induction.

The Centre was a small room lined with technical reports, training manuals and books on management. John Boulton, the Information Centre Manager, suggested a database search for recent material on environmental regulations and standards as the quickest way to gain an up-to-date picture. Within fifteen minutes I was scanning through some abstracts that John had printed out for me. As Jim and I had suspected, new regulations were proposed in a consultative document from the Environmental Protection Agency which had been given new powers. John's printout mentioned fines and penalties for breaching these controls but it did not say how much they were, or what the controls were. John said he could get me the new document by this afternoon. I also asked if he could get hold of information on managing environmental problems. There were a number of answers we needed: what was the best advice available? And what were 'proscribed substances'? I still wasn't sure that I had got all the questions, let alone the answers. At two o'clock that afternoon all the information I needed was on my desk. I phoned John to thank him for excellent service.

The consultative document was full of horrendous mumbo-jumbo. I dug through it and realized that we could be in serious trouble. It was clear that legal procedures would be instigated against organizations which made no attempt to introduce measures to reduce pollution within eighteen months. The clause on fines and penalties was an eye-opener. The maximum fine was £100,000 and there was the threat of forced closure if controls were ignored. Even more frightening was the suggestion that individual managers might be criminally liable. We had little choice in the matter; the cost of keeping our heads in the sand would be far higher than the expense of renewing our antiquated machinery.

Waiting for the results of Jim's tests, I started drafting recommendations. I knew it was crucial to point out not only the benefits to the environment but also the marketing and financial advantages of taking action before the regulations became law. The need to safeguard our image in the eyes of customers, employees and the whole community had to be emphasized and could ultimately have its effect on sales and profitability. As a final point, I indicated the personal liability for compliance which directors and managers would have.

I got Jim's results before the end of the week. As we both feared, we were over the top, badly in some cases. But the situation was recoverable if we acted at once. I now had all I needed to make some authoritative recommendations.

Is this the last lap Michael? With the input from Sue, Alan and John, a total of seven us have made contributions to the report. I've spent the most hectic eight weeks of my life on it and your help and advice have been priceless. I would like to buy you the dinner of a lifetime. Until then, thank you!

Andrew

Extract of letter from Michael to Andrew dated 27 May

. . . problems of the environment are not going to go away. Care for the environment, inside and outside the organization, is now the most neglected issue of concern to all managers. One of the answers to managing the environment is in distinguishing the key issues from the crack-brained. Advice will range from water treatment to windmill construction; the key is to recognize the dominant issues affecting United's position in the community, and adapt practical suggestions that *can* be beneficial. Let me try to summarize some of the more important aspects:

- Try to identify the wheat and the chaff. Care for the environment manifests itself in many ways. Try to separate the larger issues from the petty, and the more important from the emotive.
- Be aware of environmental legislation and standards which will provide the key to acceptable, and therefore to unacceptable, practice.
- Your early efforts should be devoted to a comprehensive audit of the organization's manufacturing equipment, raw materials, and waste-disposal processes.
- You must establish procedures to track damage levels over periods of time. These will help you to initiate measures to control that damage.
- Like all other aspects of management, environmental management needs its proper allocation of resources and responsibilities. If policies are to be effective then they need to be implemented throughout the organization. Staff education and training, and retraining, will require their own budgets.
- To be effective, staff must know that policy comes down from the top in a clear statement from the Board. If it doesn't come down from the top, then it will get lost long before it reaches the bottom.

THOU SHALT CARE FOR THE ENVIRONMENT IN ALL THAT THOU DOST

A further point:
You have already achieved much progress towards your goal, but there will still be obstacles to overcome and I sense from your letters that the pace is hotting up. As you approach the conclusion to your project, there will be ever more problems to solve and decisions to take. Do not lose faith as that last lap gets nearer. I've said before that you must know when to step back and when to compromise. Now you must also know when to take action, and responsibility for it.

THOU SHALT STRIVE TO OVERCOME WHATEVER OBSTACLES LIE IN THY CHOSEN PATH

Good luck

Michael

The Tenth Letters –
Overcoming Obstacles

Nephew

I must tell you that I received a call from a member of Infernal Security last night. The subject of our discussion, which I found extremely painful, I am not at liberty to divulge. What I can say is that when he left at midnight I felt a sense of impending doom, and that the sufferer of this doom was not me.

Whilst my lips are sealed about the subject of the visit, I can remind you of the fate recently suffered by another junior tempter who failed in his assignment. Infernal Security committed him to the hands of the Infernal Retraining and Redeployment Executive (IRRE), who condemned him to a hundred years of continuous attendance at Slake and Croutons's Managerial Griddle seminars. He was comparatively lucky; the lot of a failed junior management tempter is not to be envied. The IRRE's methods are effective, if only because they keep such individuals out of mischief for a very long time. But centuries of continuous attendance at seminars, t-groups, counselling and appraisal interviews interspersed only with continuous redrafting of the c.v. is not something I would wish on my worst enemy.

The fate of agents who fail us is even worse. They are committed to the Director of Sub-Human Resources to deliver to an Appointed Place where they are publicly stripped of their mobile phones, company cars and keys to the executive toilet, outplaced, and forcibly entered on a register of self-employed consultants. Their operation is then downsized and delayered, and the remains are finally out-sourced. I would suggest that you leave Srebmun and The Curate in no doubt as to the horrors they now face.

I found your latest attempts the most feeble yet; the memo you left on Buckden's desk was puerile and pointless. You now have what is without doubt your last chance to destroy Buckden. You must find an infallible way of checking his hitherto almost continuous progress towards management competence – some obstacle too high for him to climb, too wide for him to circumvent. Let me, as a final act of kindness, remind you of the first lesson you were taught when you entered the portals of ICM; the Seven Basic Principles of Management Frustration:

1   Starvation
2   Blocked arteries
3   Family feud
4   Act of God
5   Computer crash
6   An inspector calls
7   Moving goalposts

Let me remind you how each works.

Starvation

The best way to starve managers is to cut off their cash. This can be done by arranging a crisis at the most inconvenient moment, or by ensuring that no budgetary provision has been made for some essential need.

In Production or Sales, the supplies are physical and can be blocked by arranging for supplier bankruptcy or similar problem, delays of all kinds, or perhaps a failure to meet specification.

In other functions, whilst some supplies (e.g. paper clips or coloured polythene folders) are physical, shortage of these is unlikely to bring the operation to an immediate standstill. It is better, therefore, to block the supply of information, and this can be arranged in a number of ways; breakdown of the telephone switchboard, postal strike, simple inefficiency on the part of those whose job is to supply it. By allowing Buckden to make contact with the Information Manager, Boulton, your bungling has wasted a fine opportunity.

An amusing alternative to blocking the flow of information is to organize for it to be incorrect. Nothing is more satisfying than to see managers fighting hard on one front (preparing to increase their output, for example) when the enemy is advancing from a completely different direction (returning ever more rejects, perhaps). Provided managers are busy or stupid enough such delusions can often be maintained long enough to destroy them.

It may be possible to cut off less obviously essential supplies; computer paper, perhaps, or envelopes. We brought one medium-sized company to its knees by cutting off its supply of toilet paper, something which brought the staff out on indefinite strike. Use your ingenuity.

Blocked arteries

Because every operation is part of a 'supply chain', along which products or data must move steadily and without interruption, there is as much scope for oversupply as for starvation. Nothing is funnier than to see a manager's operation brought to a standstill by a massive delivery of unusable material, or by a customer returning the entire last six months' work as faulty.

Family feud

Managers can be destroyed by a breakdown of interpersonal relationships of almost any kind. The most effective are:

● Boardroom battle. This is not, of course, confined to the boardroom. Managers at every level spend the bulk of their time and effort in political infighting and intrigue.

The MDU promulgated the tongue-in-cheek description 'organizational culture' amongst teachers of management; the commonest organizational culture is, of course, based on back-stabbing, politicking and the vilifying of whichever of one's colleagues currently poses the greatest threat. Few business schools include this in their curriculum.

This 'culture' offers two chances of destruction; first if managers back the losing side, and second if they spend so much time and energy in feuding they have none left for other work. The first is more powerful. I am not convinced that Buckden is a skilled politician, and this could yet offer you a good opening.

- Industrial action. The use of strikes, working to rule and strife between managers and the managed may appear old-fashioned. It is true that the Shop Stewards and Works Convenors Division of the Directorate has recently been disbanded, and its ex Head is now being reprogrammed. However, the possibilities in this area are not exhausted; you should remain alert to their use. Nothing will destroy a manager more thoroughly than being seen as the cause of a strike at a crucial time.

Act of God

You may wonder what we are doing employing such an odd phrase which, as you know, is forbidden blasphemy at Tempter level. However, I am rather fond of it, conveying, as managers within the insurance industry will confirm, any event which appears destructive, random and unpreventable. We have worked hard to ensure that such happenings have not been put down to our account.

Earthquakes, lightning, flood, fire and tempest can damage any manager's career. However, there are difficulties which make such stratagems less suitable than beginners believe.

First, authority for such assistance is, rightly, difficult to obtain. I myself have to complete a detailed application form and obtain no less than five authorizing signatures in order to engage the services of a small tornado. Indeed, use of anything more powerful than a Grade

3 earth tremor is reserved to Council Members whose application is personally endorsed by a Deputy All-Lowest. You will understand that these aids cannot be for the use of junior staff.

Secondly, there is a danger that these devices may backfire, and strengthen rather than weaken the manager's position. They may generate sympathy. They may hide the evidence of mistakes. They may even, if the manager is more effective than we have judged, provide an opportunity to demonstrate their ability to overcome problems. You must under no circumstances try this approach in your attempt to destroy Buckden. He has already shown a great deal too much competence for my taste.

Computer crash

Computers are one of the two devices (the other is atomic power stations) the workings of which are not explicit, and are therefore often attributed to us. They appear to have a life of their own. (A respected earthly philosopher recently seriously suggested they were conscious.) Their correct functioning has for long been regarded as the preserve of Someone Else – namely the Computer Department, which is also seen by many as part of our Empire. When they go wrong, the results can be highly destructive.

For these reasons, computer malfunction has been an excellent way of thwarting managers' efforts. However, the introduction of desktop and indeed laptop machines, over which individual managers have considerable control, has rendered this area less fruitful.

Indeed, the boot is now on the other foot. There is a danger that, using the latest equipment, managers may learn how to increase their productivity and control to an unacceptably high level. Only yesterday, I saw a manager completing a report on a London tube train in the rush hour. He also had a portable telephone and modem, and I shuddered to think what he might achieve during his journey by mainline train. Of course, laptops can be knocked by strangers and fall to the floor, as this manager found when I rose to get out at Kings Cross. That was a particularly satisfying computer crash.

An inspector calls

Bureaucratic interference is one of the best means of ruining managerial effort, and it is good that it remains as your penultimate weapon. Few things are more destructive than the intervention of someone with power but neither understanding nor interest in the end result. Apart from the capricious and damaging nature of any instructions issued by such an individual, the time wasted in attempting to resist them, the effort necessary to try and circumvent their interference in the future, and the bad feeling caused are all of immense value to us.

This is an area in which we have made tremendous strides in the last fifty years. There is now a massive range of petty officials who have the right to enter premises with or without permission, stop a manager in whatever he is doing, demand answers and information, call for, inspect and impound documents, and impose penalties, often without recourse to courts of law and usually without effective appeal.

It was as a fledgling tempter that Blatherwyke, now Dean of the Faculty of Bureaucracy at ICM, first applied the destructive power of do-gooders to the world of management. The idea seems obvious now, but no one else had spotted its importance. He extended the approach from matters such as the import of goods without paying duty, through an ever-increasing range of taxes. The establishment of 'Value Added Tax' was, as is generally known, entirely his doing. How Blatherwyke persuaded otherwise intelligent and fair-minded legislators to adopt a method of taxation that was not only unfair but as inefficient as could be devised, is a fascinating story yet to be written. From here, he spread the blight into anything that might be regarded as affecting health or safety, i.e. anything – working at a screen, even sitting at a desk. There is virtually nothing a manager can now do which is not open to interference.

Moving goalposts

Footballers and other sportsplayers confirm that hitting a moving target is not easy. Managers spend much of their effort in trying to do this, and with the same degree of failure.

The principle is to initiate the confusion at the highest level. If the Board (or Council or whatever) changes policy frequently, or even better, has none, the chances for effective management are nil.

The way success is measured should be altered often. If strict adherence to budgetary constraints has been the criterion, replace it with entrepreneurial flair and the grasping of promising opportunities. After a while, arrange that the maximum level of production becomes the benchmark, to be followed quickly by minimum rejects or perhaps maximum number of staff training days. Apply pressure by bringing forward deadlines without explanation. Almost anything will do provided it is changed often enough, the changes are badly communicated and, if possible, conflicting standards are applied at the same time.

I suspect that this may be the best area in which to make your final throw for the career of Buckden. We know he is impatient with bureaucrats, whom he regards (rightly) as barely human. His operation covers ground which is wide open to their examination. He is already, thanks to at least some of your earlier efforts, under increasing pressure from Srebmun. I recommend you look at the possibilities with great care.

Should this final chance fail, my duty to you will have been done, and there will be nothing I can do to spare you from the attentions of Infernal Security.

It is still my wish, even now, that you escape this fate.

Barripper

Monday 8 June

NOT POSTED . . .

Dear Michael

I apologize for following up my last letter before you've had the chance to reply, but I need to write to you. My meeting with Hines was this morning. I've just come out of it – I might go back into it. It seems in any case likely to be the last I shall attend at United. This has been a most extraordinary affair so far. If I knew your phone number, I would ring you; directory enquiries told me that you weren't listed. As I don't know how to contact you, all I can do is to put this morning's events on record.

Before I say anything else I want to thank you for the support you have shown me in my brief career at United. Whatever else comes out of this time, I shall always value our exchange of letters and your uncanny help. I enjoyed the work on resources with my colleagues; we became, in the end, an effective team. Roland and I finally made some progress together, and working with Martin brought out the best in each of us. I enjoyed my hectic, last-minute research on the environment too. Anyhow, I must tell you what has just happened.

I had to cope with a series of unlooked-for hitches over the last few days. The first of these was the discovery that all the materials I needed to finish the report were out of stock; good quality A4 paper, binding material, computer disks. When I asked for an emergency purchase, I was told that Hines had put a moratorium on all cash expenditure until the end of the month. I ended up buying them in town out of my own pocket.

Next came shortage of information. I needed a number of cost figures, which Alan Bowden had promised to supply. He is the most methodical and helpful manager in the place, and I had relied on his promise to supply them. When I called at his office, his assistant told me that Hines had sent him, the evening before, as his representative to a conference in Geneva. He wouldn't be back until next Monday – too late for my report. His assistant did not know how to access the information. I rang Alan's home, and his wife told me which hotel he was staying at. I phoned and had him pulled out of the conference. He explained how I could get the information, and by eight-thirty that evening I had found it, checked it and printed it off.

You will not believe the next problem. I arrived before eight the next morning to find the drive blocked by a large delivery van, labelled 'Peters' Perfect Pencils', and the front door blocked by a stack of boxes. The driver was standing by the reception desk with a delivery note in his hand. 'Can I help?' I asked.

'Sign for these, will you?'

The note indicated a consignment of one hundred cases, each holding ten gross – a total of nearly one hundred and fifty thousand pencils.

'There's something wrong here,' I exclaimed, with righteous indignation, just as Hines struggled through the barricade. 'Who in the world ordered this lot?'

The driver consulted his documentation: 'Chap called Buckden – A. Buckden.' He showed the signature to both of us.

Telephoning a succession of ever-more senior people at Peters' Perfect Pencils, I at last got Mr Peters himself to instruct the driver to remove the cases. Before I had done so, other staff were already arriving, including Arthur who kindly calculated that, if placed end-to-end, the pencils would stretch over three miles.

I have not had time to sort this one out. If things go as I expect today, I never will. But I found it sinister that Hines did not demand an instant explanation. To add to my feeling of impending doom, Joan popped her head round the door to announce in a voice of total disbelief that Arthur Harris had just been sacked.

'Escorted to the door,' she whispered, 'Not even allowed to clear his desk.'

'Why . . ?'

'No one has the slightest idea,' she replied, and went back to my report.

Hines' secretary rang next morning. Her boss had now asked for my report by the following day; four days early. I'm convinced he was livid to learn that it was almost complete.

I came in before eight again this morning. On reading the report for the last time, I realized that I needed to make one or two adjustments to the budget figures. I switched on my micro and called up the file. It had gone. My directory had been wiped clean. I didn't believe it. Not now. Not at this stage. All of a sudden those final modifications became the difference between life and death. I asked Joan to find out if there had been a network crash in the night. There hadn't. Joan must have thought me crazy as I rushed home for my back-up disks. Nothing was going to wreck all the work I had done. I made it home in record time and got back to make the final changes with ten minutes to spare.

I knew that if things went wrong this could be my last day with United Group. I had blotted my copybook twice already with Hines; we still had to discuss the little matter of the pencils. I tried to compose my thoughts by chatting with Joan. It relaxed me a little, but I still felt like a man about to put his head on the block.

I arrived in Hines' outer office bang on time. I wasn't going to allow myself to be wrong-footed from the start. As soon as I saw him, I felt he was under some kind of pressure, although I could not make out what it was. He spoke fast, often through clenched teeth. At intervals he glanced anxiously at the door and then at his watch.

He started to work through my report. The section on cost-saving and the use of resources hardly seemed to interest him, even though it had been the basis of the whole exercise. He asked no questions, made no comments, but homed in rapidly on the environmental section. He picked up what he called the 'astronomical cost' of implementing the changes needed to meet the new environmental regulations. He managed to make it sound as though it were my fault. I was resigned to this, knowing he would take this line. I reminded him that, unless we made the necessary changes, it would only be a matter of time before our operations became illegal. He clearly took that as a threat, but I stood my ground. I pointed out that it would be in our interests to start the work as soon as possible, before we were compelled to. He asked why this had come so late in the day and why the organization was not better prepared. I said it might be because no one in the organization was directly responsible for environmental matters, that it was a new area, and that it was probably a case of everyone thinking that someone else was doing it.

I sensed him moving up a gear as he suggested that I appeared keen to meddle in others' affairs, and accused me – as Roland had done – of empire-building. I wasn't to be browbeaten. I argued that if someone else had it under control, I would not have duplicated their work.

He returned to the resource proposals and stared at the report's signatures. Looking up, he said: 'Is it your intention to be subversive Mr Buckden? I told you not to involve others until I'd seen your proposals.'

I was sure that he hadn't said that but it didn't seem to matter. I sat in silence, wondering whether there was any point in answering his question. A phone rang. Hines nearly jumped out of his skin. I could tell that he was listening to the conversation his secretary was having with the caller in the outer office. Hurriedly, he dug into a drawer and threw a paper in front of me. I recognized the purchase order for pencils.

No words were necessary. I couldn't believe what I was seeing. It was my writing – my signature. I checked the details, and the penny dropped. My request for one box of pencils for Joan had been changed to one hundred cases. I showed him the alteration.

'Whether there has been such an alteration, I am not qualified to say,' he said, with even greater pomposity than usual. 'But I would like to know whom you believe would have done such a thing?'

Once again, I was at a loss for an answer that I was prepared to give. My list of suspects would certainly be headed by his own name. But the final blow was still to come.

'Whilst you are considering your reply on that point, perhaps you would care to examine this photograph.' He handed me a colour print of Sue and myself trying to leave the Dog and Duck, apparently deep in each others' arms. 'You know the company policy on relationships between staff, I presume?'

For the third time, I had nothing to say. My moment had come. There was a knock, Hines jumped from his seat, and almost ran to the door. Rising, I saw the MD, Lady Grazier, with a stranger in the outer office.

'Give us a few minutes, will you, Mr Buckden?' said Lady Grazier.

Hines said nothing, but stood with his back to me as I walked out.

(The letter breaks off at this point. What follows was gleaned from discussion between Andrew and Laura later that day.)

I walked back to my office in total confusion. What was going on? Who was the stranger? I felt I knew him. Hines was clearly expecting him. Why was the MD there? I thought I might as well collect my personal belongings together. I found a cardboard box. While I filled it, I thought about my report. I knew it was good. I also knew that change was what United Group needed and my colleagues agreed with me. It wasn't change for the sake of it. There had been too little change, or rather, not enough progress. Now change was needed in large doses. I sat at my desk and tried to place the stranger. I was sure I'd seen him before.

I'd just got to the end of writing down these last strange events when my phone rang. It was Hines' secretary. In a slightly odd voice, she asked me to come back up. When I entered her office, she looked at me strangely, and said. 'Mr Temple will see you now.'

Inside, sitting in Hines' chair, was the stranger. As he looked up at me smiling, I recognized him.

'Why, Michael! What in the world are you doing here?' I came near to embracing him – if the desk had not been between us, I think I would.

'Mr Hines has left the employment of United Group. I have taken his place.'

'You mean you are the new Comptroller?'

'Yes.'

'How . . ? Why . . ?'

'I can make no comment about Mr Hines, why he has left us, or where he has gone. You will have to make your own judgement about that. What I can say is that the MD and I wish to thank you for your excellent report. The suggestions you make on managing resources in United Group are long overdue and the work you have initiated on the environment will prove essential to our survival.'

'You mean you've read it already?'

'Yes.'

'But Michael, the letters – the checklists – all the things I wrote about the Company and the people in it?'

'Andrew, I don't know what you're talking about. But I do understand the stress you have been under in the last few weeks, and this morning in particular. I suggest you take a few days' leave. You have won your spurs as a manager.'

'Arthur Harris . . . Did you have anything to do with his disappearance?'

'No, that was Hines. I understand there was a breakdown in essential office supplies; the clamour was too great even for Hines to ignore. In the strictest confidence, Andrew, there also were unexplained alterations to expense claims and purchase orders. However, that's enough for now, I think. We've both had quite a busy last few days. When you return from leave, I suggest you begin by giving some thought to a revised description of your job; you'll have a lot to do implementing the recommendations in your report.'

I left his office in a daze. Back in my own, I unpacked the cardboard box. To my amazement, Michael's letters were not in it, where I was sure I had placed them. I never saw them again.

In the End

These letters raise a number of questions.

Did Andrew and Laura marry and live happily ever after? Were Sue and Alan promoted? What are the present market projections for plastic elephants? Was Hines liquidated, or did he set up as a management consultant? Will Harris' role as a double agent entitle him to two pensions or none at all: Is Michael Temple related to a previous Archbishop of Canterbury, or is he an under-cover executive of the Management Charter Initiative? We know that Barripper lives on to attempt to drag other managers to destruction, but what actually did happen to Relubbus? We have an instinctive belief that the answers to these questions will somehow be made manifest to you before too long.

The letters also provide a number of important answers. We now know why, as managers, we have always felt persecuted and unappreciated. We have a new understanding of the phrase 'management development'. If we suddenly start receiving regular checklists from a comparative stranger, we will view them in a different light.

But most of all, the substance of the Ten Commandments and their associated checklists has burnt into our souls. Despite not being delivered through the usual channels, they seem to us, as disinterested observers, both wise and helpful and we recommend them to your study and use. With them, your future in management must be assured – at least until the next round of downsizing.

The Ten Commandments of Management

(As revealed to the Authors on Kinder Scout, Derbyshire, England, in November 1991)

1 THOU SHALT ORGANIZE THYSELF AND SET A GOOD EXAMPLE TO OTHERS
2 THOU SHALT SET OBJECTIVES AND PLAN WITH CARE
3 THOU SHALT BOTH GIVE AND RECEIVE COMMUNICATION EFFECTIVELY
4 THOU SHALT KNOW AND SEEK TO SATISFY THY MARKET
5 THOU SHALT STRIVE TO USE ALL THY RESOURCES WELL
6 THOU SHALT THINK CREATIVELY AND WELCOME NEW IDEAS
7 THOU SHALT MONITOR AND CONTROL THE PROGRESS OF THINE OPERATION AGAINST THY PLAN
8 THOU SHALT LEAD THY PEOPLE AND HELP THEM DEVELOP TOWARDS THEIR FULL STATURE
9 THOU SHALT CARE FOR THE ENVIRONMENT IN ALL THAT THOU DOST
10 THOU SHALT STRIVE TO OVERCOME WHATEVER OBSTACLES LIE IN THY CHOSEN PATH